The Spirit

The Spirit of Witness

*Liturgies, Prayers, Poems and
Reflections for Dissenters*

Martyn Percy
Emma Percy
Jim Cotter
Heather Carter
Rebecca Parnaby-Rooke
Dave Lucas

with

The Ordinary Office
Los Olivos Retreats
The Church of the Holy Family, Blackbird Leys

CANTERBURY
PRESS
Norwich

© The Contributors 2023

Published in 2023 by Canterbury Press
Editorial office
3rd Floor, Invicta House,
108–114 Golden Lane,
London EC1Y 0TG, UK

www.canterburypress.co.uk

Canterbury Press is an imprint of Hymns Ancient & Modern Ltd
(a registered charity)

Hymns Ancient & Modern® is a registered trademark of
Hymns Ancient & Modern Ltd
13A Hellesdon Park Road, Norwich,
Norfolk NR6 5DR, UK

British Library Cataloguing in Publication data

A catalogue record for this book is available
from the British Library

978-1-78622-445-3

Typeset by Regent Typesetting
Printed and bound in Great Britain by
CPI Group (UK) Ltd

Contents

Birth and Baptism

United in Love

Suffering Presence

Death and Resurrection

About the Contributors

The Revd Heather Carter is Minister of the Church of the Holy Family, Blackbird Leys, Oxford. The church is a designated Local Ecumenical Project and under Heather's leadership provides extensive outreach and support to the community.

Jim Cotter was an Anglican priest and wordsmith whose prayers, psalms and hymns enabled many to forge a new spirituality. Writing and speaking for nearly 50 years, he developed a network through Cairns, a publishing enterprise he began in the 1980s. In his spiritual writings, he described the challenges of being gay and latterly his battle with leukaemia (which led to his death in 2014 at the age of 72). His personal story, particularly his bouts of depression, helped others to come to terms with their life, sexuality, suffering and spirituality. He described his ministry as 'free-range': quiet prayer, simple hospitality and thoughtful conversation.

The Revd Canon Dr Robin Gibbons is a Melkite Priest (Catholic, Eastern Rite) and is a teacher and writer in the Department of Continuing Education at the University of Oxford. He is also an Ecumenical Canon of Christ Church Cathedral, Oxford.

David Lucas is the founder of 'The Ordinary Office', an online church community based on Twitter with a weekly service on YouTube. Raised a Catholic, he discovered a new sense of God through his two guide dogs, Abbot and Jarvis. David is an activist lobbying churches to change their attitudes to disability and inclusion.

The Revd Dr Daniel Muñoz is an Anglican priest and theologian with a particular interest in exploring the intersections between art, poetry and Christian spirituality. He is the chaplain of Los Olivos Retreats in Spain.

Rebecca Parnaby-Rooke is a writer and music therapist. She co-leads the inclusive online community 'The Ordinary Office' and has published in the online devotional library 'Our Bible App' and in the short-story compilation 'Queer Hands of God'.

The Revd Canon Dr Emma Percy is an Anglican priest and theologian. She writes and teaches on practical feminist theology and ministry studies and is a former Chair of WATCH (Women and the Church).

The Very Revd Professor Martyn Percy is an Anglican theologian and priest. He writes and teaches on faith, culture and public life, and also on the sustainability of churches in contemporary culture.

Introduction: Witness in Ordinary Time

MARTYN PERCY

You would be forgiven for thinking that this book might be another about witnessing and how to pass on your faith to others. You may be familiar with that genre of Christian writing – lots of stories, techniques, handy hints and encouraging tips. If so, you will be disappointed. This is not that sort of book. Indeed, we hope the subtitle has given you a clue as to what to hope for.

Witnessing to the truth, to the Spirit and to Christ is about something far more important for Christians. True witnessing is usually found in dissenting. No, we won't bow to idols. Nor will we take the easy road. No, we will not seek safety. Nor will we turn from the cross. No, we will not deny Christ or any and all he died for. Nor will we exclude those who harm and hate us. Christian witness dissents. Our faith is not conformed to the world. Having the mind of Christ mostly means we are bound to do things differently.

'Witness' is a term that has become synonymous with evangelism and it has been tamed, domesticated and emasculated by successive generations of Christians in modern times. It has come to mean something that is either written or spoken by some and then done to others. As though folk could be persuaded by a cogent argument or slicker presentation. It has become a hobby for specialists; for brave souls, a somewhat trivial pursuit implying eager and enthusiastic enterprise; a sort of practice that everyone can have a crack at but is otherwise optional. So much so, in fact, that we can pay for others to do that which we either can't or won't do ourselves. I ask you, who would be a Christian witness? I mean, *seriously*?

As I say, this is not that kind of book. Perhaps like you, I am rather wary and weary of any more offerings on improving techniques for sharing the gospel. If the key to evangelism lay in slicker presentation, or clearer or cleverer explanations, then we would have discovered this long ago. In truth, we are evading what we already know, deep down. That is this: to be a witness – a true one – costs everything. It is fundamental to our being Christian.

In this short collection of poems, prayers, reflections and liturgies, we have sought to express the witness of dissent with contributions that are not stamped with any approval, authorization and licensing by the Church. You will find liturgies and prayers for lovers, civil partnerships, bereaved parents mourning an infant, racism and Gay Pride. Our poems and reflections are intentional exercises in dissent, so that we can recover authentic Christian witness from the clutches of a safety-first, risk-averse faith. True witnessing causes trouble; it questions the worldly powers and religious authorities. Witnessing requires courage, care and kindness. None of these are for the timid.

Our old English word 'witness' meant 'attestation of fact or an event' and 'from personal knowledge'. Just as we use the term in legal proceedings, the witness is 'the one who so testifies'. There is an older word – hardly used now – which is 'inwit', and our forebears used this as a synonym for the mind or seat of thought and consciousness. While we use the English word 'wit' for humour, our forebears understood 'wit' to mean the human intellect and moral reasoning.

We only find the residue of this meaning in old phrases such as 'at our wit's end' or being 'scared out of our wits'. Neither of these phrases is about the loss of humour. In the past, 'common wit' meant common sense – or the things we could all be sure of. By extension, 'inwit' was internal knowledge, and to 'outwit' someone was to confound them with wisdom or knowledge. There was even something called 'clean inwit' – the pure 'thoughts of the heart' that we find are invoked in Thomas Cranmer's majestic collect, where we are invited to petition for purity in our wits and witness.

Christian use of the word 'witness' is, in fact, more demanding than purity of the mind and heart, and purity of knowledge. For early Christians, witness meant death – the very term was a literal translation of Greek *martys* from which we get the word martyr. My own name, Martyn, is a derivative of this. You could say I was Christened to suffer. But I am not a masochist. Every Christian is called to suffer with Christ; to share in his com-passion; to die to ourselves, and with Christ, in order to be raised by God. We are witnesses to this.

A witness on the witness stand in a court of law is someone (hopefully) speaking the truth, as though their life depended on it. We are forbidden to bear false witness against others: this is the ninth of the Ten Commandments. A poor witness in a trial is someone who cannot give a good account of their testimony, or becomes confused about what they saw, heard or did, or might be unable to answer questions succinctly and clearly. As a verb, witnessing meant to 'bear testimony', and legally to affix your name or signature to a document or testimony to establish your identity, or the probity and provenance of a claim. It also meant to see or know something, by personal presence, and to observe.

The first Christians were witnesses. They bore testimony; they personally saw and met with the resurrected Jesus; they were prepared to be martyred for that, and to lose their lives as their saviour had done. A true Christian witness signs their own death warrant: they die to the world, and are alive to Christ; they share in the sufferings of Jesus, even to death; they are pointers to signs of a life that is no longer theirs but God's.

True witnesses are bound to be convicted by their own testimony. They cannot be freed by what they say, or do with their lives. Christians, as witnesses, are committing themselves to a future as convicted ones – witnessing to truths and life that the world has never shirked from condemning, or even crucifying.

The Scriptures give us many kinds of witness. The eager-yet-still-confused-and-sore-afraid. The ones with conviction. The ones who need more convincing, like the apostle Thomas. The ones who see, yet do not believe. They are also witnesses. Mary the mother of Jesus is a witness to God, to hosting the Holy Spirit within her, and to the gestation of the Son of God. She witnesses to the death of her son too.

No mother should have to bury their child. Joseph too is a witness and must hold his tongue at being cuckolded by the Holy Spirit.

He must witness to Jesus growing up, knowing he is not his biological father. Zechariah can only witness to his son, John, with a pen and paper. When he writes the name of his son, only then may he speak again – to witness. Elizabeth witnesses to Mary's pregnancy, with her guts (Greek *koilia*) or womb 'leaping' or somersaulting in anticipation of this other birth.

The shepherds and the wise men witness. So do the angels. Herod is a bad witness, as he will not want to affirm a newborn monarch on his turf. The consequence of this is that hundreds of parents will, in turn, witness the massacre of their children. We will never learn of their testimony, but we can imagine it. Such slaughter is surely a life sentence – every birthday of every infant remembered for decades to come. Candles lit, absence mourned, perpetual pain, unresolved grief. Perhaps some will dare to conceive again. Perhaps the birth of a child after the cruelty of such carnage will be a new witness to life and love, which death cannot rob from the bereaved.

Jesus has many witnesses. John the Baptist might be the first to lay a claim on this for the adult Jesus. Yet John is more than aware that the witness of the Holy Spirit at the baptism of Jesus trumps his. The Spirit witnesses to the Son; the Son witnesses to the Father. Why does this matter? If I am right, and witnessing is the cost of discipleship to every Christian, every day, then we should rethink our place in the world and the calling of the Church. The Church is not about attraction to others, or fear and anxiety about its retraction. The Church is a witness: the sign that Christ died, was raised and will come again. In power, and in glory, to judge the living and the dead. We signed up for this – to testify – when we became Christians. Indeed, this is everything we have to witness.

William James, one of the first psychologists of religion, often asked what actions a belief resulted in; or, as he put it, what its cash value was, or its benefit to believers. When investigating a religious claim, he would advise his readers and students to ask, in what *facts* does this belief result? For James, beliefs were the grammar or rules for action, and their test was the practical consequence of holding them. So let me give an example here.

If you believe that God rewards fidelity and fervent prayer with health, wealth and prosperity, the signs of that belief will be manifest in material riches and well-being. Lack of faith will manifest itself in illness and poverty. If you believe in the inherent superiority of white people to all other ethnic groups, it will inevitably lead to acts of discrimination against all non-whites. For William James, the outcomes of these forms of witness or testimony could not be clearer. That is why all Christians should reflect with care on our beliefs and subject them all to the Jamesian test: what are the practical consequences and benefits of holding particular beliefs; in what actions do they result?

The early Christians, as witnesses, could answer as follows. To be a witness was to testify to Jesus, who was himself a witness to God. Jesus was and is the Witness. The Light had come into the world: the darkness did not comprehend it. When the true Light of the world dawned, most people preferred the darkness. So they simply extinguished the light – Jesus was snuffed out for them, so to speak.

But God raised up Jesus and the Witness continues to be alive now, and we are witnesses to that. It followed, therefore, that the early Christians saw their witness as a literal sharing in the death of Jesus: martyrdom for the faith. Bearing witness meant signing your life away. Being prepared to be convicted by your own testimony. But this was a testimony of 'clean inwit' and 'pure outwit' – inner thoughts and desires cleansed, and outer works confounding the spirit of the age with a wisdom and practice that seemed to the world folly.

The early Christians undertook all manner of works that had no reward, nor even obvious results in which they could delight. They cared for the widows, the orphans and the marginalized. They looked after lepers. They witnessed to Jesus, who was himself a witness: the literal body language of God in time and space, living with boundless compassion, mercy, grace and love. The Witness was as God is; and the early Christians were called to *be* 'like-wise'.

'Like-wise-ness' is an integral aspect of being a Christian. We are called to be Christ-like. Our like-wise-ness is meant to be one of resemblance in actions, virtues, character, forbearance, courage, hope, love, compassion and suffering. We are invited into imitating the love of God for others, and most especially the alien, marginalized and neglected. The early history of this is brought to life vividly by John Boswell in his book *The Kindness of Strangers: The Abandonment of Children in Western Europe from Late Antiquity to the Renaissance* (New York: Pantheon, 1988).

The early Quakers picked up the tempo and testified to the light within everyone – the inward light – and the inherent dignity of all humanity. It led them to minister to the prisoners, to serve their fellow humans in all spheres, and even when their pacifism forbade them to fight they would nonetheless volunteer for the most dangerous medical missions in frontline conflict. As Abraham Heschel, the Jewish scholar, puts it, 'there are no proofs for the existence of the God of Abraham – there are only witnesses'.[1] Note: 'only witnesses'. There is nothing and no one else. Just us.

Dietrich Bonhoeffer also testifies that 'God is the beyond in our midst'[2] – and so can only be met in the face of the poor, naked, prisoner, hungry and stranger. How should we live as witnesses? Not, I think, in a permanent state of anxiety about numerical church growth or numbers of converts. The Church is often called to dwell in exile, and the experience of forced deportation and dislocation is rarely a time of abundance or popularity.

The Church, like Jesus, is constantly subject to ostracism and expulsion. The Church is for outcasts. But the Church itself is cast out for precisely such endeavour. The first Christians were ejected from their places of worship – synagogues. They were rejected in their communities. They were worshippers, in turn, of the one who had been despised and rejected. Christians live in a constant state of both conviction and eviction. If the world is not trying to dismiss, exclude and disown the faithful, we will have over-befriended our culture and context and lost our purpose. A popular and bulbous church has to work hard not to become unfaithful in its obesity and swollenness.

The activist Dorothy Day wrote:

> To be a witness does not consist in engaging in propaganda or even stirring people up, but in living the mystery; it means to live in such a way that one's life would not make sense if God did not exist.[3]

The early Christian martyrs saw themselves first and foremost as witnesses. They did not see themselves so much as persecuted, as they were imitating Christ. Stephen, the first martyr and therefore the first Christian witness, died embodying his faith through his purposeful acts. His death was in many respects pointless. Surely, he could have argued that his work was socially valuable, charitable and for the common good. Why did he die, exactly?

The account of Stephen's death in the book of Acts is striking, not least because the manner of his death and surrender is consistent with his life – a surrender of himself to care for others who could not take care of themselves. His witness was against a social ordering and hierarchy that permitted this blasphemy, and the moral indignation that led to his death was, of course, a protest at his witness. If Stephen's moral world prevailed, then too many people had too much to lose. There would be a level playing field. The poor would be enriched. The enriched would share with the poor. His witness was in his death, but also in his life. His devotion to the poor was a witness to the culpable neglect of his time. His care shamed the inaction of others. His non-aggressive resistance, with its firmness and fidelity, did not evade the violence that destroyed him.

There are other kinds of witness too. In many respects, poems, reflections and meditations that are in this book are intended to help us think more deeply and even more intensely about the nature of witness.

For example, there are reflections on marriage and family life. Marriage requires witnesses. But to what do we witness when we attend a service of matrimony, and who enters into any marriage? The original meaning of 'to wed' comes from the stem root of 'to wage' – as in something precious like money, one's life or future. We often fall into the trap of assuming that 'Christian marriage' has a settled history and tradition and it is only recently that other forms of commitment have been recognized and granted sacralized sanction. Nothing could be further from the truth.

So I have deliberately included material in this volume that is about the witness of all marriages – male–female and same-sex. I hold that every union of true and mutual love will bear some testimony to God and witness to the love of Christ and the power of the Holy Spirit, in grace, generosity, abundance, openness, kindness and humility. The Scriptures are clear on this: 'God is love, and those who abide in love abide in God, and God abides in them' (1 John 4.16b).

We moderns might be shocked by the (hardly opaque) enjoining of couples to 'join giblets', which was as much a proposal as a statement about a union. Likewise, 'to tie the knot' was a literal reference to binding the hands of a couple together, with the guests often having material of the same type or colour as that of the bride, and witnesses keeping their own knotted ribbon or fabric in joining hands as a lucky charm. 'Getting hitched', 'fastening', 'buckling' (note symbolism) and 'yoking' were all commonplace terms for marriage.

I am persuaded by the writings of John Boswell (see *Same-Sex Unions in Pre-Modern Europe*, New York: Random House, 1994) and Alan Bray (see *The Friend*, Chicago: University of Chicago Press, 2003) who identify the patterning of love and fidelity in same-sex unions going back many, many centuries, as signs, testimonies and witnesses to the love of God living within loving unions.[4] In the same way, other kinds of union – say, the fraternity of monks in a monastery – witness to other kinds of loving union and communion.[5]

Love is where God chooses to be most manifest: radiantly, gloriously, fully. Witnesses in the Scriptures take many forms. Moses before the burning bush is a testimony that compels witness, long before comprehension of what was seen and heard can be understood. The signs of Jesus in the Gospel of John are witnesses, and John begins and ends his Gospel with meditations on witnessing.

The Word was with God, and the Word was God – from the beginning. That Word becomes flesh in Jesus, and John concludes his Gospel by explaining that there have been so many signs and testimonies attributed to Jesus, the Gospel cannot contain them all. Witnessing is a boundless endeavour and it has no ending.

John's Gospel sees witnessing as forward-looking, but also propelled from the Word as the source of life, who was and is from the beginning, before all things were made. John the Baptist – who is another contender for the first witness to the life and ministry of Jesus – is primarily a witness to the judgement and justice of God. The witness of John the Baptist also points us to the witness we must all bear in the life of the Holy Spirit.

However, I have always been fascinated by the witness of others. By 'others' here, I mean the uncanny ways in which God uses outsiders to remind insiders that they don't possess all the truth; that any smugness in our faith and conviction will be confounded, always, by the God of surprises. The Scriptures are full of illustrative tales of the alien and the stranger bearing the message of salvation back to the faithful, who invariably don't want to know it, hear of it or do anything about it. The good Samaritan (Luke 11), Cyrus (Messiah, Isaiah 45) and the Gentiles are all less-than-subtle prods from God that the Holy Spirit is alive and present beyond the frontiers of organized religion and clubby fellowship. God is bigger.

We would do well to remember this, as our world is not divided between rationality and religion, sacred and profane, poetry and science, or myths and reality. Humanism, as many scholars have testified, from the early Greek philosophers such as Aristotle through to the Renaissances of knowledge in Arabia, China and Europe, and several religious Reformations across Europe, might be less about destroying God and faith, and much more about humanity and how it might be saved. We can go further here and say that, like good religion and many a mystic and metaphysical poet, we all know – somehow – that we cannot be saved alone.[6]

Every civilization and culture that has not tipped into an abyss of despair has tended to invest in predictions and prophecies of dazzling futures for humanity. Some of these futures can be social, material and economic; others, technological, moral or perhaps, like Nazi aspirations, eugenic. Religious and spiritual presumptions concerning the future are hardly alone in the panoply of forecasting. Many faiths presume that they can evolve and grow exponentially. This is what Mary Midgley terms 'one of the long myths' we live with as humanity.[7]

To call such forecasting a 'myth' does not mean that it is a false story. Myths are stories that are true on the inside but not necessarily factual on the outside. Myths are the tales and tropes we live by that carry great symbolic power, and live independent of their truth. In our vision-scoping for the Church, the setting of objectives and prophecies of growth and abundance have such symbolic power. But these tales and tropes are living quite independent of the truth that they relate to. That is why it is so important to work with our plain common sense.

Otherwise, the myths cloud our thinking and we fall into the abyss without even experiencing a second of the despair that might have made us pause. It is not that myths are bad, per se.

It is just that if we 'live-by-myths-alone' (to corrupt a biblical phrase), we can't really be shocked and surprised at the end results.

As Jean-Paul Sartre says: what is not possible is not to choose. We need to think more carefully about the nature of the kin-dom of God in which we work, live, move and have our being. If we simply opt for myths and phantasies of growth, then we will lose sight of other things that are intrinsically valuable. Our values matter.

As parents will know, at least instinctively, if you opt for only grooming the physical intellectual abilities and skills of your children, they'll miss out, quite by accident, basic social components like developing a sense of humour. It is hard to teach people to laugh. Harder still to teach how important to us it is to have some other qualities, such as emotional warmth. Miss these two things out of our curriculum for raising children and, without really meaning to do so, we can easily stumble into producing people with deep coldness. Such a possibility seems utterly unimaginable, and yet it would be entirely predictable.

There is an obvious question to ask here: 'How and what do our children witness to their parents?' We are all products of nature, and of nurture. We are witnesses to how we were born and raised. As Henri Nouwen asks us:

> Can I give without wanting anything in return, love without attaching any conditions? Considering my immense need for human recognition, I realise it will be a lifelong struggle. But I am also convinced that each time I step over this need and act free of my concern for return, I can trust that my life can truly bear the fruits of God's Spirit.[8]

Margery Kempe was a fifteenth-century mystic and probably the first woman to write an autobiography in English. She struggled, as many English people do, with 'sweaty semi-Pelagianism', our almost unique national heresy that believes we must do a bit more to earn God's favour. There is always more you could do to earn salvation; never stop sweating and working for that end; God does not really care for slackers. So, work harder. That's why I love this gentle antidote that she wrote down, revealed to her: 'More pleasing to me than all your prayers, works and penances is that you would believe that I love you.'

Kempe was right. The Gospels also confirm that Jesus was quite keen on slackers. Jesus had this knack of rewarding ten lepers with healing, not just the one who was grateful. Jesus told parables about labourers in vineyards who were well rewarded for not a lot of work, if any. Salvation is not a loyalty-reward-card-bonus-scheme like you might find at your local supermarket. Jesus gives rewards to people who are not members of any scheme and, for the record, are not able to pay their way or have much of a clue about the relationship between loyalty and bonuses.

What would it take for the Church to witness to that kind of love? The truth is, we don't allow ourselves or our churches to go there, because we are desperate to be liked, and so we create endless schemes and wheezes that seek to recruit. But the Church is not that attractive (seriously, take a look), and in this new millennium is in exile. Maybe if we grasped our exilic situation better and berthed ourselves in authentic core values and truth-speaking, we'd be less inclined to sell ourselves short. True, exile has its down side: it is displacement and expulsion, and it is invariably alien and painful. But as Eugene Peterson asks, 'Exile always forces a decision: will I focus my attention on what is wrong with the world and feel sorry for myself? Or will I focus my energies on how I can live at my best in this place I find myself?'[9]

It would take more than this book to answer such questions. But we have tried to make a start, and with poetry, prose, homilies, reflections and prayers, we are issuing a simple invitation to you, the reader. Namely, to think again about your life as a witness, and the ways in which witnesses have in turn crafted you – through their grace, graft and goodness. In this, try to see this world anew as God sees it, acting as Jesus would act, and if you can, make your mark of witness only that.

Several of the sermons, talks and homilies in this volume are drawn from preaching to ordinands at Cuddesdon or to the congregation at Christ Church Cathedral, Oxford. Readers will appreciate that context always counts in preaching, and the selected texts are chosen for their resonance with the theme of witnessing.

Notes

1 Abraham Heschel, *The Prophets*, vol. 1, New York: Harper & Row, 1962, p. 22.

2 Dietrich Bonhoeffer, *Letters and Papers from Prison*, vol. 8, Minneapolis, MN: Augsburg Fortress Press, 2010, p. 367.

3 Robert Coles, *Dorothy Day: A Radical Devotion*, Reading, MA: Perseus Books, 1987, p. 160.

4 John Boswell, *Same-Sex Unions in Pre-Modern Europe*, New York: Random House, 1994; Alan Bray, *The Friend*, Chicago, IL: University of Chicago Press, 2003.

5 See also Patrick Riley, *Civilizing Sex: On Chastity and the Common Good*, Edinburgh: T & T Clark, 2000.

6 On this, see Mary Midgley, *Beast and Man*, London: Routledge, 1979.

7 See Mary Midgley, *Evolution as a Religion*, London: Routledge, 1985.

8 Henri Nouwen, *The Heart of Henri Nouwen: His Words of Blessing*, ed. Henri Nouwen, Michael J. Christensen, Rebecca Laird, Chicago, IL: Crossroad Publishing, 2003, p. 33.

9 Eugene H. Peterson, *Run with the Horses: The Quest for Life at Its Best*, Downers Grove, IL: IVP, 2019, p. 29.

WITNESS IN
ORDINARY TIME

Witnessing is one of the central callings for followers of Jesus.
Yet this sometimes means bearing witness against the Church
itself. It has meant, and still can, bearing witness against an
oppressive state, injustice, cruelty and inhumanity. Our calling
can be to bear the witness of prophetic prosecution, or of
the disciples in their defence of the gospel. A witness testifies
to the truth of what they have seen, heard and experienced.
They must be prepared to be cross-examined, to proclaim,
to be questioned, to be truthful and courageous – but also to
have the humility to accept that they may be wrong in what
they thought they saw, or what it meant. We remember that
the first witnesses to the resurrection did not 'see' anything,
much less understand it. In this, we are promised the Spirit of
Witness, the Holy Spirit to guide us into all truth, as we speak
and embody what we know. Witnessing is not about being
certain. It is, rather, about being open to what God says to us,
through us and around us. It takes time to discern. For every
minute we speak, and for every word we write, may we spend
far more time listening to what the Spirit of Witness is seeking
to teach us.

Liturgy

THE ORDINARY OFFICE

A prayer for witness

Peace to those who want to witness, yet have to turn away.
Jesus witnesses for you, and loves you for your intent.
Peace to those who want to help, yet don't have the resources
to do so. Jesus knows your heart, and loves you for it.
Peace to those who wrestle with big emotions, of fear, grief,
sadness, anxiety, pain and loss. Jesus holds your suffering,
and loves you through it.
Peace to those who feel nothing is ever enough. To Jesus, it is.
We are loved by the creator of the stars, the author of a
multitude of human epic tales and the composer of a million
bird songs. In our weakness we call on Her, and in doing so
we find our strength.
And may the peace that comes with the knowledge of that
strength reside with you today and always, by the Spirit left
with us, in Jesus' name. Amen.

A blessing for those who witness

God sees you, you who hold up the traffic in desperation to
show the world Gaia cannot face another decade of plunder.
Lay down your weary arms and be blessed.

God sees you, you who work daily seeing images of children
no person should create, to save more from being created.
Close your weary eyes and be blessed.
God sees you, you who take your medication every morning
and donate the little functionality it gives you to campaigning
for others who don't even give that much. Rest your weary
body and be blessed.
God sees you, you who minister within your Church, with
a front-row seat to humanity and decreasing capacity to
bear the unbearable load. Lay down your weary collar and
be blessed.
God sees all, hears all and knows all. Lay all down at the foot
of the cross and be blessed.

Quiet day at home: Morning Prayer

Jesus said: 'I am the light of the world.
Whoever follows me will not walk in darkness,
but will have the light of life.'

Silence

O God, open our lips
and our mouth shall proclaim your praise.

Blessed are you, loving God, our beginning and our end,
to you be glory and praise for ever!
From the rising of the sun to its setting,
your life and your love fill every corner of the earth.
Fill us with your Spirit afresh this day,
that we may walk the road less travelled together
and by your grace reveal your presence in the world.

Creator, Redeemer and Giver of Life:
blessed be God for ever!

God calls us to love one another:
O come let us worship.

Looking for my Love,
I will walk through these mountains, by these rivers,
I will not pick the flowers, nor will I fear the beasts,
and I will cross through fortresses and borders.

O forests and deep thickets, planted by the hand of
the Beloved,
O meadows of green pastures,
painted with colourful flowers!
Tell me if he has passed by you.

Pouring a thousand graces he hurriedly passed by these groves
and after looking at them, solely by his presence
he clothed them with his beauty.

The night has passed and the day lies open before us.
Let us pray with one heart and mind.
As we rejoice in the gift of this new day,
so may the light of your presence, O God,
set our hearts on fire with love for you and others,
now and for ever. Amen.

The reading for the day

Matthew 5.1–12

Silence

For the word of the Lord,
thanks be to God.

Prayers

The virtuous soul that is alone and without a teacher is like a lone burning coal; it will grow colder rather than hotter.

Show yourself to us at the break of day.
Lord, have mercy.

The soul enkindled with love is a gentle, meek, humble and patient soul.
May your loving kindness fill the earth.
Christ, have mercy.

A tree that is cultivated and guarded through the care of its owner will produce its fruit at the expected time.

Hear our cry, O God, and listen to our prayer.
Lord, have mercy.

Other prayers

This is the day that God has made,
we will rejoice and be glad in it.

We will not offer to God,
offerings that cost us nothing.

Go in peace to love and to serve.
We will seek peace and pursue it.

In the name of the Trinity of Love,
God in community, holy and one. Amen.

Quiet day at home: Evening Prayer[1]

When evening comes you will be examined in love.

As we approach the evening and the night,
may God grant us a quiet evening and a perfect end.
Amen.

My friends, brothers and sisters,
our help is in the name of the eternal God,
who is making the heavens and the earth.

Blessed are you,
God our light and our life,
to you be glory and praise for ever!
When we turned away
to darkness and chaos,
like a mother you would not forsake us.
You cried out like a woman in labour
and rejoiced to bring forth a new people.
Your living Word brings
light out of darkness
and daily your Spirit
renews the face of the earth,
inclining our wills to the gentle rule of your love,
Creator, Redeemer and Giver of Life:
blessed be God for ever!

A period of silence follows for reflection on the past day

God, for your love for us, warm and brooding,
which has brought us to birth and opened our eyes
to the wonder and beauty of creation,
we give you thanks.

For your love for us, wild and freeing,
which has awakened us to the energy of creation:
to the sap that flows, the blood that pulses, the heart that sings,
we give you thanks.

For your love for us, compassionate and patient,
which has carried us through our pain,
wept beside us in our sin
and waited with us in our confusion,
we give you thanks.

For your love for us, strong and challenging,
which has called us to risk for you,
asked for the best in us and
showed us how to serve,
we give you thanks.

Reading from Scripture

Matthew 5.1–12

Silence

For the word of the Lord,
thanks be to God.

Lord, now you let your servant go in peace:
your word has been fulfilled.

My own eyes have seen the salvation:
which you have prepared in the sight of every people,

a light to reveal you to the nations:
and the glory of your people Israel.   (Luke 2.29–32)

Glory be to you, Creator, Redeemer and Spirit of Life:
as it was in the beginning is now and shall be for ever. Amen.

Let us bless one another, saying together:
The Lord bless us and watch over us;
the Lord make his face shine upon us and be gracious to us;
the Lord look kindly on us and give us peace. Amen.

Notes

1 Sources for this quiet day are: The Anglican Church in Aotearoa, New Zealand, and Polynesia, *A New Zealand Prayer Book (He Karakia Mihinare O Aotearoa)*, San Francisco, CA: Harper, 1997; J. Philip Newell, *Each Day and Each Night: A Weekly Cycle of Prayers from Iona in the Celtic Tradition*, Glasgow: Wild Goose Publishing, 1994; *The Iona Abbey Worship Book: Liturgies and Worship Material Used in the Iona Abbey*, Glasgow: Wild Goose Publishing, 2004; *St. John of the Cross: Ascent of Mount Carmel, Dark Night of the Soul, and A Spiritual Canticle of the Soul and Bridegroom Christ*, ed. Paul A. Boer Sr, London: CreateSpace, 2013.

Poems – Five Witnessing Women

EMMA PERCY

*These poems emerged out of a retreat at Los Olivos (Spain)
led by the Revd Dr Erica Longfellow. The retreat provided
a rich environment to pray, reflect and write, and the author
expresses her gratitude for all those who came, and for the
space and leadership the time gave her.*

Julian of Norwich

*Julian of Norwich (1343–c. 1416), also known as Juliana
of Norwich, Dame Julian or Mother Julian, was an English
anchoress of the Middle Ages. Her writings, now known
as* Revelations of Divine Love, *are the earliest surviving
English-language works by a woman, although it is possible
that some anonymous works may have had female authors.
They are also the only surviving English-language works by an
anchoress.*

*Julian lived in the English city of Norwich, an important
centre for commerce that also had a vibrant religious life.
During her lifetime, the city suffered the devastating effects
of the Black Death of 1348–50, the Peasants' Revolt (which
affected large parts of England in 1381) and the suppression of
the Lollards. In 1373, aged 30 and so seriously ill she thought
she was on her deathbed, Julian received a series of visions or
showings of the Passion of Christ. She recovered from her illness and wrote two versions of her experiences, the earlier one*

*being completed soon after her recovery, and a much longer
version, today known as the Long Text, which was written
many years later.*

*Julian lived in permanent seclusion as an anchoress in her
cell, which was attached to St Julian's Church, Norwich. Four
wills are known in which sums were bequeathed to a Norwich
anchoress named Julian, and an account by the celebrated
mystic Margery Kempe exists which provides evidence of
counsel Kempe was given by the anchoress.*

*Julian's writings emerged from obscurity in 1901 when a
manuscript in the British Museum was transcribed and published with notes by Grace Warrack. Julian is today considered
to be an important Christian mystic and theologian.*

Dame Julian, you contained yourself
voluntarily incarcerated in a simple cell,
removed from social niceties
and the requirements of a conventional life.
And from your restricted space
your mind was freed to explore,
travelling the heights and depths of revelation,
weaving a theology both traditional and yet radically
    your own.
Here sin and pain call forth the compassionate gaze of
    the Creator
and find in our Mother Jesus a redemption rich and generous,
through which we shall be oned with the one who made us,
so that all shall be well,
not a pious platitude but a triumphant assertion
of the overwhelming capacity of God's redeeming love.

Margery Kempe

Margery Kempe (c. 1373–1438) was an English Christian mystic, known for writing through dictation The Book of Margery Kempe, *a work considered by some to be the first autobiography in the English language. Her book chronicles domestic tribulations, her extensive pilgrimages to holy sites in Europe and the Holy Land, as well as her mystical conversations with God. She is honoured in the Anglican Communion but has not been canonized as a Catholic saint.*

Kempe was an orthodox Catholic and, like other medieval mystics, believed that she was summoned to a 'greater intimacy with Christ' as a result of multiple visions and experiences she had as an adult. Kempe did not join a religious order, but carried out 'her life of devotion, prayer, and tears in public'. Her visions provoked her public displays of loud wailing, sobbing and writhing which frightened and annoyed both clergy and laypeople. Kempe met the mystic Julian of Norwich on a number of occasions and claims to have conversed with her over several days.

Kempe was tried for heresy multiple times in her life but never convicted; she mentions with pride her ability to deny the accusations of Lollardy with which she was faced. Possible reasons for her arrests include her preaching (which was forbidden to women), her wearing of all white as a married woman (that is, impersonating a nun) and her apparent belief that she could pray for the souls of those in purgatory. Kempe was also accused of preaching without church approval, as her public speeches blended her personal faith with commentary on Scriptures.

Margery, who from the pains of psychotic devilry
found salvation in the loving gaze of Christ.
You searched for a life of holiness
struggling against expectations of husband and home,
of clerics and bishops,
limited by what a woman could be,

what a woman could know,
what a woman could say.
You searched for validation from those considered learned,
considered wise, considered holy.
Your tears, your emotional neediness and your
    un-learned visions
caused others to dismiss, dislike, distrust and disempower you.
Yet, God in Christ knew you,
validated your desire to speak,
sustained you in the courts of heresy.
And so you found a voice and left a tale to be told
of a woman of faith, a woman of grit, a woman of God.

Teresa of Avila

*Teresa of Avila was born Teresa Sánchez de Cepeda y Ahumada
and lived from 1515 to October 1582. Teresa, who had been a
social celebrity in her home province, was dogged by early family
losses and ill health. She was also a Spanish noblewoman who
was called to convent life in the Catholic Church. A Carmelite
nun, prominent Spanish mystic, religious reformer, author, and
theologian of the contemplative life and of mental prayer, she
earned the rare distinction of being declared a Doctor of the
Church. Active during the Catholic Reformation, she reformed
the Carmelite orders of both women and men. The movement
she initiated was later joined by the younger Spanish Carmelite friar and mystic John of the Cross. It led eventually to the
establishment of the Discalced Carmelites. In her mature years,
she became the central figure of a movement of spiritual and
monastic renewal born out of an inner conviction and honed
by ascetic practice.*

Teresa, you knew what you wanted
and used your gifts to achieve it.
Playing the authorities, side-stepping censure, trusting in God.
Practical in the worldliness of notaries and financiers,

treading the fine line of inquisitorial acceptability.
Sockless, you created communities of equality and austerity
where women could think and pray,
where women could move beyond the telling of beads
into the exploration of spiritual mansions,
where women could move through ecstasy
into the full contemplation of the divine.

Anne Askew

Anne Askew (sometimes spelt Ayscough or Ascue; married name Anne Kyme; 1521–46) was an English writer, poet and Anabaptist preacher who was condemned as a heretic in England during the reign of Henry VIII of England. She and Margaret Cheyne, wife of Sir John Bulmer, who was similarly tortured and executed after the Pilgrimage of Grace in 1537, are the only women on record known to have been both tortured in the Tower of London and burnt at the stake.

Anne is also one of the earliest known women poets to compose in the English language and the first Englishwoman to request a divorce, especially as an innocent party on scriptural grounds. Askew was a devout Protestant, studying the Bible and memorizing verses, and remained true to her belief for the entirety of her life. Askew met other Protestants, including the Anabaptist Joan Bocher. Askew stuck to her maiden name, rather than her husband's name. While in London, she continued as a gospeller, or preacher to all. Askew's quick mind and brilliant memory for Scripture infuriated her torturers. When requested to divulge the names of other like-minded women, she responded: 'God hath geven me the gyfte of knowledge, but not of utterance. And Salomon sayth, that a woman of fewe words, is a gyfte of God' (Sirach 26.14).

Anne, what led you into the church to read the word of God?
Defying the law, turning the pages,
speaking the words of Scripture in a woman's voice.

What courage you displayed as those words learnt by heart
became your foil against your accusers.
I cannot comprehend the faith that sustained you as they
broke your body.
I want to turn away from the breaking and burning,
your costly martyrdom so oft forgotten in the telling of our
Church story.
May we not forget you, our courageous foremother,
as we stand in our churches and speak God's word in
women's voices.

Amelia Lanyer

*Emilia Lanyer (also Aemilia or Amelia Lanier, 1569–1645;
née Aemilia Bassano) was the first woman to assert herself
as a professional poet through her volume* Salve Deus Rex
Judaeorum *(Hail, God, King of the Jews, 1611). Lanyer was
baptized Aemilia Bassano at the parish church of St Botolph,
Bishopsgate, in 1569. Her father was Baptiste Bassano, a
Venetian-born musician at the court of Elizabeth I. Her mother
was Margret Johnson, possibly an aunt of the court composer
Robert Johnson. Lanyer's family was Jewish or of partly Jewish descent. Following her mother's death, Lanyer became the
mistress of the First Baron Hunsdon, a Tudor courtier and
cousin of Queen Elizabeth I. Hunsdon was 45 years older than
Lanyer. When the relationship ended, Lanyer married a distant
cousin, Alfonso. But she often opined that she preferred being
a mistress to being married. She is regarded by many scholars
as a proto-feminist. When Alfonso died in 1613, Amelia set up
a school to educate poor children. She died aged 76.*

Amelia, married into respectability
when your pregnant body was no longer fitting for your
courtly lover.
You took courage from those strong Old Testament women,

who were not afraid to name and negate the power of
    sinful men.
Meditating on the Passion of your Saviour
you penned an impassioned defence of our foremother Eve.
Why should women be blamed for a sin that was shared?
And if women are so weak was not Adam more to blame?
And was it not men who bear the even greater sin
of condemning our Lord to die?
Four hundred years on we cry with you,
Then let us have our liberty, our equality,
our freedom from an assumed male sovereignty.
Still tainted as Eve's daughters by the Church,
we join with you in calling for the recognition of our
    full humanity
beloved of God, image bearers of the creative Divinity.
Speak to us across the years as women and as men,
sons of Adam and daughters of Eve
equally God made, equally by love redeemed.

Lady Anne Southwell

*Anne Southwell (née Harris; born at Clerkenwell in 1574),
later called Anne, Lady Southwell, was a poet. She wrote a
variety of works including political poems, sonnets, occasional verse and letters to friends. In 1594 she married Thomas
Southwell of Norfolk at St Clement Danes in London, and
they had two daughters. She became Anne, Lady Southwell,
when Thomas was knighted in 1603. She remarried after his
death but retained her name and title as Lady Southwell. She
died in 1636 at Acton, London.*

Lady Anne Southwell, with what exquisite penmanship
you craft your righteous anger towards the sons of
    blokish Adam.
Those who make themselves our heads to keep women
    from healing,

who pontificate, in earnest or in jest,
on whether women really do have souls.
You challenge us to find the souls which God gave all
and resist those who, through envy and through fear,
label prophetic women witches, wise women dull
and those attuned to the sad injustice of our world as mad
    and foolish.
So long ago you bade us take heed
that beyond this mortal life
'there will not be a difference in your sex'.
Lady Anne,
lend us your wit as we encounter those who seek to keep us
    in our place,
lend us your faith as we seek to find our wise prophetic voice.

The Parable of the Sower

EMMA PERCY

Some of my earliest memories are of going to church. This was a wonderful medieval church on the edge of a market town in Essex. You entered through a large porch and got that church smell of slight damp, old books and so on. As the Venite was sung, I would file out with the other children to the Sunday school where, with the help of crayons, plasticine and coloured paper, I learnt Bible stories and sang simple songs which taught me that I could be H-A-P-P-Y because I was L-O-V-E-D by God. And that if I was lost Jesus would find me, if I messed up Jesus would forgive me, for I was his child and I would be cherished.

When I was eight, life changed drastically; my parents' marriage had crumbled and we moved with my dad to the suburbs of London, replacing the open fields with endless pavements. Instead of an ancient church we walked up to the red-brick Edwardian parish church with none of the aesthetic beauty or ancient smell, but the stories and the songs were the same and I was reassured that though I felt very lost, though I was uncertain about whether I was loved by those individuals who were meant to love me, God could be depended on and Jesus loved me and would hold me, providing a sense of security and peace in the midst of troubled waters.

As I grew up, this faith that I had first learnt in Sunday school stayed with me. My intellectual questions became more sophisticated and my exploration of the Bible stories and trad-itions I had learnt became more nuanced. Yet none of this changed that basic core sense that I can rely on God and can know myself to be beloved, for I am in Christ.

One of the stories I learnt from my earliest days was the parable of the sower. I have drawn it, acted it out, sung action songs about it and heard countless sermons and talks on it. Yet, as I grew up it began to be a parable that I found deeply troubling. The implication in the way it was often told to me was that the different soil types bore some kind of responsibility for what they produced and increasingly this seemed to be unfair. Why was it, I wondered, that the stories, songs and sustenance of the faith I learnt as a child had given me strength through my childhood where others experiencing similar difficulties had felt the lack of God's presence and subsequently had a lack of faith? Why didn't many of my friends believe? For me it had never been a particularly difficult choice; there was no conversion experience – as one longstanding friend commented, it just took. The seeds sown bore fruit, so was I lucky to have fertile soil? Could I take any responsibility for that, and if not, was this all rather unfair? Why did faith come so easily to me and not to others?

This is a theologically deep question which touches on questions of grace, freedom and predestination. I experienced faith as a gift but that made me feel somewhat guilty for those who did not have it. Pondering on the passage it seemed to me that there could be no condemnation for those who bore little fruit due to such unproductive land. Paths are created because people trample across that piece of land, they are literally downtrodden. Brambles and weeds are virulent and vigorous and, as many of us who have struggled with ground elder or the terrible Japanese knotweed know, sometimes you need quite radical solutions to combat them. Rocks are heavy to lift. In the circumstances of some people's real lives, believing that God loves them and trusting in that may not be easy.

Two different insights helped me to look at this passage in a more hopeful way. First, Rowan Williams pointed out that those with an agricultural background listening to Jesus telling the story would have been bemused or amused by the sower's recklessness with the seed. Good farmers do not toss the seed around in such a random way so that some is wasted by falling on the poor soil. Careful troughs are created in the good soil and seed is carefully sown in the places where it will grow. The sower in Jesus' story is recklessly liberal in the way he chucks the seed around. If we see the sower as God, then we need to make sense of this liberal generosity which borders on foolishness. If we are to be like the sower, then we too need to be liberally generous even towards those who seem to have little likelihood of giving us a return. This needs to make an impact on our understanding of mission and growth in the Church. We are not to restrict our 'giving' only to the places where we are likely to succeed. There is something about continuing to sow in the unproductive places knowing that they will be unproductive that is at the heart of God's mission.

The second insight came from a children's book written about a different parable. Nick Butterworth and Mick Inkpen have written short illustrated versions of eight parables. In one, the story of the wise and foolish builders, on the last page you see the house on the rock standing and in it are both men, while out on the line hang the wet clothes of the man whose house on the sand was washed away. I found this simple illustration deeply moving. The one who had put his faith in Jesus is able to offer hospitality to the one who had not.

Returning to the parable of the sower, I note that the seed that falls on good soil produces a large amount of grain, 100, 60, 30 times what was sown. This plentiful crop can provide food for many, so perhaps as in that previous illustration we can recognize that the fruit that comes from the good soil is meant to be shared generously, not least with those whose circumstances are very different: the downtrodden, those choked by the cares of the world, those blinded by the injustices around us.

Those of us who have been gifted with faith, with a capacity to believe in God, to trust in Jesus and know that peace which passes understanding, have riches to share with those for whom such faith is hard to comprehend. Those of us who know what it is to be held by the love of God, sustained by the compassion of Jesus through the ups and downs of life, have strength and comfort to offer to the downtrodden, storm-tossed and thirsty people who experience life as chaotic and unjust. We share the gifts and strengths of our faith to sustain and support others in the work of the people of God in the world.

And our faith enables us to bring into God's presence those who would perhaps find it too difficult to get there on their own. I recall one of the highly regarded Grubb Institute training courses on leadership, roles and personhood. On this particular course, the late (and great and woefully under-rated) Ian Tomlinson was one of the principal facilitators of the group work. Some clergy mentioned their anxieties about low numbers in their congregations and the decline in church attendance. I was one of these clergy. Ian sat back and said that he thought hundreds of people went to our churches and that we were not counting properly.

We were baffled. But as Ian explained, one person brings many – in their heart, mind and prayers, each day, each and every week. Just one person attending would bring dozens of people before God. Our faithful bring many. He added that some people will be extremely surprised when they arrive in heaven and discover how often they were in church.

So, if you have faith, then use its fruits generously. Feed the hungry, comfort the afflicted, work for the downtrodden, and when you come before God bring others with you so that your faith may be a rich resource bountifully feeding God's people.

Truth was Given

EMMA PERCY

Truth was given,
a thing of beauty, soaring up on sunlit wings,
sweeping down to rest in my hands,
but this, I am told, is a no-fly zone.
Here truth must be contained,
the status quo maintained.
Words must stay unspoken,
bonds must not be broken,
certainties unshaken,
liberties not taken.
So I contained the truth.
At night she flew around my room keeping me from sleep.
In the day, held close, she beat against my heart
and flew into my mouth longing to be free.
It hurts to be restrained,
for hope to be detained.
Truth should be outspoken,
the bars that bind, broken.
Complacency shaken,
initiatives taken.
For the truth shall set you free
when truth herself is freed
and the uncaged bird allowed to sing.

A Blessing

THE ORDINARY OFFICE

Peace to those who respond as impossible calls inspire their hearts. For faith will be rewarded.
Peace to those who wait in wonder for stars to guide their path at night. For faith will be rewarded.
Peace to those who do what must be done, journeying on while bearing precious burdens. For faith will be rewarded.
Through responding, through journeying, through following the guide we have in our Holy Spirit, may we always find our faith rewarded as we learn more about Jesus, drawing closer to Almighty God. Amen.

Prayer for Peace in Ordinary Time

THE ORDINARY OFFICE

What do we do, when peace is so fleeting and conflict so rife around us?

Look to the sky. See the soft, rolling clouds and watch the gentle movement of the earth. On and on it turns, in a constant, life-giving path. Know it turns to give you the sunlight you need, and the darkness to rest. That is how much God loves you.

Look to the earth. See the green shoots, abundant in the country or persevering through the cracks in urban space. On and on they grow, in a constant, life-giving effort. Know they grow to give you the air you need, and to clean the air in turn. That is how much God loves you.

Look to your heart. See the space within where the Spirit lives, rests and resides in you. On and on God works, in a constant, life-giving endeavour. Know God is always there, purifying, pruning, gently weaving the strings of your heart together with God's own in a beautiful braid. That is how much God loves you.

Feel the peace that comes with the knowledge and understanding that this is how much God loves you.

Amen.

Peace be with you.

COMMUNION

Communion is one of the central acts of Christian worship. Jesus' body broken and blood shed is the re-enactment of God's complete and total love and commitment for humanity and the world. It is a meal. It is a sacred-social event that reminds us Christ was born for us, lived for us, died for us and was raised for us. It is for sharing, because God in Christ is shared among us. In turn, God asks us that this feast becomes an extended invitation to offer to the wider world. Communion with God may be solitary, and it may be shared. But it is never private and personal. As we feed and are nourished, so are we to feed the world with the same love, grace and tokens given to us. In these liturgies, sermons and poems, we explore communion as gift-sharing. For us, and for all.

Beware the Leaven of Christians

MARTYN PERCY

How do you get dough to rise? We moderns are used to yeast in small packets and in plentiful supply. Much modern bread manufacture depends on it. I use the term 'manufacture' here with precision, and as someone with some personal knowledge of how modern, mass-market sliced bread has, these days, become the main kind of bread that we find in our supermarkets.

For some people in the Church, the name Chorleywood will be synonymous with the New Wine Network, Vineyard Churches, John Wimber, Barry Kissell, John Perry, David Pytches and Mike Pilavachi's ground-breaking Soul Survivor festivals. Few of the residents, I am guessing, will have noticed, tucked away behind a high wooden fence on a main road, the Flour Milling and Baking Research Association headquarters, or heard of the invention of the Chorleywood Bread Process (CBP).

After the ravages and rationing of World War Two, feeding Britain was not easy. So the Ministry of Agriculture, Fisheries and Food turned to research that could produce bread on a mass scale – ideally cheaply and with a long life. Chorleywood Bread Process helped develop forms of bread that were quick to make and fast to bake, lasted a long time, and were inexpensive. The sliced white loaf seen in all supermarkets is the legacy.

The Chorleywood Bread Process used dry-packed yeast. It represented a quick, reliable, predictable, mass-market and inexpensive rising agent. But for many people, this is not 'real' bread at all. Rather like the campaign for real ale, there has been a marked turn in the closing decades of the twentieth century, continuing into the twenty-first century, that has sought to recover the authentic texture, taste and nourishment of real bread. Of course, it cannot be mass produced and so it is normally more expensive. But the difference between a manufactured loaf and an artisan one is as night and day, or chalk and cheese.

So, to the key question: how many times does the word 'yeast' get used in the New Testament? The answer may surprise you: none. The New Testament gives us around a dozen occurrences of the Greek word *zýmē*, and although many Bible translations will render that word 'yeast', the actual word is for 'leaven'. You may be forgiven for thinking the difference in translation – as we might say of the yeast itself – is tiny. Indeed, small beer? I don't agree.

The word yeast comes from the old English word 'gist' or 'gyst', and ultimately from an Indo-European etymological root simply meaning yes. But that 'yes' also grew to mean to boil, foam or bubble. Put another way, yeast is the ingredient that turns the passive into active; the flat into flavoursome; the ordinary into the extraordinary. However, yeast, as a discrete entity and distinct ingredient, would have been completely unknown in the kitchens and households that Jesus inhabited. Bread was not made that way; nor wine, nor beer.

The world of the ancient Near East made varieties of flat-breads and sourdough loaves. With no yeast to hand, leaven was the only rising agent. True, and in some respects, super-ficially, it performs a similar task to yeast. Leaven (used as a noun) is a substance added to dough to produce fermentation and our English word comes in part from the Latin *levamen*, which in literary use meant 'alleviation and mitigation' but in colloquial and everyday use had the literal sense of 'a means of lifting; something that raises'. It is from the root *levare*, mean-ing 'to raise', and it has passed into our usage to describe the act of enabling something to 'not be heavy', or to seem to 'have little weight'.

As a noun, 'leverage' is a related term – lifting and influencing – to the verb leaven. Leavening and leaven-ous activity excite fermentation in dough or wine, and the term has come to mean something more figurative: the sense of 'work upon by invisible or powerful influence'. When we read the Gospels, we assume that Jesus' use of the term is broadly critical, say, of the Pharisees – that their leaven is a cipher for the spreading influence of something concealed; a coded symbol for the spreading nature of evil. Most translations render the Greek word *zýmē* as yeast, but as I have already indicated, the bread of the world 2,000 years ago was either a flatbread or a version of what we know today as sourdough.

There are other reasons to persist with translating the Greek *zýmē* as leaven, and not as yeast. In Luke 13.21 (parallel Matthew 13.33), leaven is compared to the rising agency of the kingdom of God. So Jesus alerts us to the good aspects of leaven. Compare Matthew 16.6, 11, however, and we are warned off the 'leaven of the Pharisees' (see also Mark 8.15 and Luke 12.1). Paul, writing in 1 Corinthians 5.6–8, renders positive uses of leaven, as does Galatians 5.9. In each case, the use of leaven, whether in making wine or bread, requires knack, know-how, skill, care, calculation, experience, trial and error, labour and patience.

If I make one aside here, it is in relation to 'gyst', which we discussed earlier as yeast, but discounted as helpful. GYST is a modern mnemonic, meaning 'Get Your Stuff Together' (sometimes rendered 'Get Your Shit Together') and is closely related to 'get your act together'. The agency implied in the mnemonic is: get up, get organized and get busy. Don't stand around or dither; sort out your life and start living it usefully. It has also come to refer to our own completion of critical end-of-life planning issues, such as gathering essential documents like wills and letting your children know where to find your bank details – but only after you have died. In other words, leaven might have something to do with our organized legacy.

That brief aside has one value, namely, to ask what is it, exactly, that is quite so *bad* about the leaven of the Pharisees?

To answer this, one has to understand how sourdough is made. Before we had active dry yeast or instant yeast, our forebears used wild yeast. We still have wild yeast, as it literally lives *everywhere* – in the air, in a bag of flour and on the surface of fruit such as grapes.

Modern domesticated commercial yeast replaced wild yeast for most of our baking because it's easier for companies to mass produce, and it was far easier for bakers to store and use in proofing our breads and pastries, all done in a fraction of the time and a fraction of the cost.

A sourdough bread gets its flavour from wild yeast that is naturally found in your kitchen. This of itself may not sound interesting, until you begin to appreciate that a San Francisco sourdough will taste different from a New York one, or from one made in an artisan bakery in Oxford or London. Real sourdough has the authentic leaven that evolves from its micro-environment, and that will be distinctively contextual.

Leaven for bread is made by trusting in the natural process of the spores as they are mixed with flour and water. Leavening in sourdough is made from a mixture of flour and water; after a day or two, bubbles will start to form in the starter, indicating that the wild yeast is starting to become active and multiply. To keep the leaven happy, it is 'fed' with fresh flour and water over several days, until the starter mix becomes bubbly and billowy. Once it reaches that slightly frothy, billowy stage, the starter is ready to be used for kneading. The mixture becomes a playground for lactobacilli bacteria and wild yeast. These naturally occurring organisms work together to catalyse the leavening, and rising properties occur: the complex flavours and textures then emerge in the baked loaf.

So when Matthew 16.6 (NASB) records Jesus saying to the disciples, 'Watch out, and beware of the leaven of the Pharisees and Sadducees', what exactly are we looking out for? Superficial translations and expositions that opt for 'yeast' will quickly render the meaning of the text as a warning against narrow-minded religious exclusivism and sectarianism.

Of course, that could mean many things, but as leaven is

meant, not yeast, then we have to accept that the leaven Jesus speaks of is everywhere, and that includes the kitchens and homes of all believers. And like bread, any believer of any type can be half-baked, over-baked, burnt, undercooked, puffed up or dead flat. I am not sure, in other words, that 'leaven' is an exclusive problem for Pharisees. I think you find bad leaven in any faith and any branch or flavour of it. You can meet mild and accommodating fundamentalists and zealous hard-line liberals.

As we all need leaven, and it is actually unavoidable (there is no good bread or wine without it), it is reasonable to infer that Jesus' association of the word leaven with the Pharisees and Sadducees might imply some level of corruption. Caution should be exercised, however, in assuming that corruption is only to be found among the Pharisees and Sadducees. Leaven was and is unavoidable and, used wisely and judiciously, powerfully good as a rising or fermenting agent. What could be so *bad* about the leaven of these Pharisees and Sadducees?

I think the answer may lie with making real bread. There may be something implied about the quality and quantity of leaven. Bad leaven could result in a loaf that failed to rise. It could make a sourdough loaf too sour. It could make a loaf too crumbly and crumby. Or too doughy and claggy, so difficult to chew and eat, and unpleasant to digest. Too much or too little leaven in a loaf will lead to a loaf that is puffed up, too full of air pockets or too dense and hard.

The character of the local leaven itself is also an issue. In local yoghurt making, some of the micro-cultures that continuously produce significant yields of natural homemade yoghurt were made (or begun) decades ago. Leaven, likewise, is not necessarily made fresh, and many trusted 'starters' for sourdough loaves are derived from leaven that can have begun its life many years ago. So a corrupting leaven would continue to produce bad bread. There is something here, therefore, about the potential legacy of the leaven of the Pharisees and Sadducees.

So I think our best way of reading Jesus' references to leaven is to imagine the outcomes after kneading and baking has taken place. That returns us to the Flour Milling and Baking Research Association headquarters at Chorleywood. True, we aspire to catholicity and unity, but Christianity was never meant to be a religious version of the Chorleywood Bread Process – exactly the same loaf, tasting exactly the same, wherever you are.

Christianity, like theology, is local and it must take on some of the distinctive character of its context in order to be faithful to the authentic calling to be incarnational – embodying Christ and loving the world in the time, space and place in which the gifts and fruits of the Holy Spirit are nurtured and developed to share with the world in gift and sacrificial service, and feed the body of Christ each and every week.

Put another way, just imagine Jesus saying: 'Pay attention to the leaven of the Christians.' What would that mean? It would imply something about all the good things that Christian leaven can do: an agent for raising and lifting up; of blessing and feeding; of being sacrificially consumed in order to feed and nourish others; to be like Jesus, Bread for the World.

To be the 'leaven of Christians' might say something about legacy and heritage; it would have plenty to suggest about being distinctive, flavoursome and local – 'this bread, here, tastes and smells beautiful, and how we wish we could take home the recipe'. When we do so, of course, it never tastes quite the same, and can't. But it can taste different, and yes, even better than we remembered as we savour it. The leaven has to be as natural as possible. We have to trust that the bubbling and frothing come in their own time. We don't use pre-packed dry yeast.

Then again, perhaps the 'leaven of Christians' would be something to warn off others. Christianity has its own pedigree that has drawn on the earlier leaven of the Pharisees and Sadducees. As churches, we have excelled at narrow-minded bigotry and sectarianism. We have been aloof and lofty and taken condescension to new heights (or depths). We have managed to talk about one bread, one body, one faith, one Lord, but then been racist, sexist, homophobic and classist.

Yes, we have plenty of bad leaven in our faith. We have

produced hard, stale, inedible faith that only a few will bite on. We have produced flaccid, flat, sentimental piety. Our leaven has also produced loaves that are so puffed up they appear to be enormous, only to find that once you try and tear off a hunk it is all air. It is best to beware of leaven.

Leslie Hunter was the Bishop of Sheffield from 1939 to 1962 and in his book *The Seed and the Fruit*, he offers this parable:

As the threats of war and the cries of the dispossessed were sounding in our ears, humanity fell into an uneasy sleep. In our sleep we dreamed that we entered the spacious store in which the gifts of God to humanity are kept, and addressed the angel behind the counter, saying: 'We have run out of the fruits of the Spirit. Can you restock us?' When the angel seemed about to say 'no', we burst out: 'In place of violence, terrorism, war, afflictions and injustice, lying and lust, we need love, joy, peace, integrity, discipline. Without these we shall all be lost'. And then the angel behind the counter replied, 'We do not stock fruits here. Only seeds'.[1]

For seeds and fruit, perhaps, we should read leaven and the loaf.

Jesus might just as easily have said, 'You are the leaven of the dough', just as he has invited Christians to be 'the salt of the earth' in Matthew 5.13. Incorrectly, Bible translations often render this saying of Jesus as salt or seasoning for the world; but in fact Jesus speaks of earth as in soil, and the *halas* (Greek: salt) would have been dug out of the shoreline of the Dead Sea, as it was rich in minerals. The ancients used it in cosmetics, but most especially to nourish the ground, as it made excellent fertilizer.

Christians are therefore to be as fertilizer: dug into the ground to nourish the soil for seeds, growth and harvest. We are invited to be a significant (if small) agent of transformative change in a much, much larger mass, which is only transformed by giving itself, sacrificially, to something bigger. Fertilizer, like leaven, does its work when it gets kneaded and worked in.

You can leave the spiritual-temporal chemistry to God. Trust me on this, the Holy Spirit knows how to bake; just remember you are an essential ingredient in God's recipe. You are no good to anyone in a jar or a packet. Christians need to get out more: we are not here to try and coax a few ever-wary people into our cupboards, containers and crocks. We were always meant to be poured out. Liberally.

How will you and I be able, like Christ, to become bread for the world? What is this leaven inside you raising up for the kingdom of God? How is Christ, in you, bringing about good 'leverage' in the world: tipping things up and toppling some other things over, or lifting and levering some things up so others can reach up, over, under or beyond? How are we, as Christ's leaven, influencing the world around us for the common good? How are we fermenting blessing, dissenting, resisting, rescuing and saving the world, and with gentleness, kindness, goodness, hopefulness, justice, peace and truth?

In what sense does our leaven *not* look like that of the Pharisees and Sadducees? Can our work upon society by 'invisible or powerful influence' be truly what Christ would be doing here, right now, in the places and spaces he has placed us?

How will you and I be part of Christ's bread for this world? How will this leaven of Christ within us now feed the hungry, house the homeless, clothe the naked and draw near to the prisoner? How will we become the body language of God; the verb of God; the bread of life for those who are hungry and ache and long for all the goodness that some good leaven can do?

Note

1 Leslie Hunter, *The Seed and the Fruit*, London: SCM Press, 1953, p. 12.

The Body of Christ

EMMA PERCY

Jesus' body was a male body,
a Palestinian Jew, circumcised on the eighth day,
muscled from manual labour, weathered by an
    itinerant ministry.
The body of Christ is black hands,
calloused from work in the fields, clapping a rhythm
    of praise.
The body of Christ is the tired feet
of the nurse at the end of the day entrusting the sick to the
    mercy of God.
The body of Christ is the foreshortened arm
offering hospitality, reaching far beyond the physical
    limitations.
The body of Christ is the breast full of milk which suckles
    the child,
the womb which bleeds and contains new life.
The body of Christ is eyes, blue, green, brown,
looking with compassion on the poor of the world,
ears that hear the voices of the voiceless.
The body of Christ is the mind
capable of exploring the heights and depths of theology,
the voice that speaks blessings in many languages,
the laughter of companions,
the sighs of lovers, the silence of contemplation.
The body of Christ is male and female and intersex.

The body of Christ is straight and gay, single and married,
    old and young, rich and poor, lost and found.
The body of Christ is risen and redeemed,
a multiplicity of human diversity working together for
    the kingdom.
We are the body of Christ, for in one spirit we were all
    baptized into that one body.

Bread for the World

MARTYN PERCY

I first saw Caravaggio's *Supper at Emmaus* at the National Art
Gallery in London when I was eight. I had an aunt who was an
artist and art teacher and, being the only member of her family
remotely interested in art and books, I was the convenient
excuse for a trip to any new exhibition. I don't remember what
we were supposed to be seeing that day, but I do remember
being profoundly captivated by Dutch Masters, Flemish scenes
and this extraordinary painting.

My aunt was a one-off. She had been an early member of the Cavern Club in Liverpool, had heard the Beatles play before they were famous and when they still had Pete Best and Stuart Sutcliffe in the line-up. She had gone on two dates with John Lennon – at the time, a student with her, studying at Liverpool Art College – and they were only memorable for being unmemorable. She liked to shop locally for food near her flat in Paddington, and I have a vivid memory of her cooking rare lamb steaks and sweet potatoes with spinach. For a northern lad, this was all new – and delicious. I liked the Beatles too, so my aunt and I had plenty to talk about.

Caravaggio (1571–1610) paints in the Baroque style and the *Supper at Emmaus* was painted in 1601. The painting depicts the moment when the resurrected but incognito Jesus reveals himself to two of his disciples in the town of Emmaus. Hitherto, Jesus has walked alongside the disciples (presumed to be Cleopas and Luke), and the conversation hinges on the body of Jesus that is now missing from the tomb. The stranger – the incognito Jesus – is prevailed upon to stay for supper with the two disciples. At which point, he reveals himself 'in the breaking of the bread'. As he does so, Jesus vanishes from their sight. The disciples then hurry back to Jerusalem to tell the other disciples.

Anyone who has seen any of the paintings by Caravaggio will be instantly struck by their sensual, carnal, even voluptuous overtones. Caravaggio is unsparing in the signals he sends to us. We see this in the painting, lush, ripe fruits, some perfectly broiled and roasted poultry, the soft human skin of Jesus, which is almost boy-like.

Caravaggio has even gone to the trouble of giving Jesus an exceptionally close shave – there is no beard to be seen, and some have seen this as a nod to the reference in Mark's Gospel account of the resurrection: 'he appeared in another form to two of them' (see Mark 16.12).

Caravaggio's fondness for the human form – which was of course manifested in his own colourful sexual proclivities – was often directly translated into depictions of food. So this supper has at its centre a bowl of fruit containing pomegranate, a ripe pear, apples, grapes and dates, with some vine leaves clearly visible. The connection between the vine leaves and the wine at table hardly needs explaining: the vine (Christ) is at the centre – and the picture literally branches off into the disciples, spreading them out (John 15.5) as his branches.

Caravaggio's private and public life was also dominated by violence and this was interwoven with his sexuality and personal life. I note this here only to draw your attention to just how animated the characters are around Jesus. Luke (left of picture) is on the edge of his seat and practically in the act of bounding out of his chair. His posture is, literally, gripping. Cleopas (right) has a scallop shell affixed to his tunic – the sign of a pilgrim and therefore of journeying. For an inanimate painting, there is much movement. The disciples are shunted, almost pushed, to the edge of the picture as Christ's right arm reaches out over the table to bless the meal. Like the world these apostles knew, the basket of food in the immediate foreground teeters precariously over the edge.

Sharp-eyed observers of the painting will see beyond the roasted bird and notice that Jesus' hands hover in blessing over not one but two loaves. His left hand drawn close to his body is over one loaf, and his extended right hand is in an obvious gesture of blessing over the second loaf. One Lord, two loaves? What is going on here, and what does Caravaggio intend us to see?

The two loaves are almost certainly challah bread, a traditional kind of Jewish loaf or cake. It can be made with eggs, and even spiced or fruited, but the loaf is also known as 'pierced bread', on account of a cut of the dough being set aside for tithing and ceremonial occasions such as Shabbat and major Jewish holidays (but note, not the Passover).

According to Jewish tradition, the three Sabbath meals (Friday night, Saturday lunch and Saturday late afternoon) and the two holiday meals (one at night and lunch the following day) each begin with two complete loaves of bread. This 'double loaf' commemorates the manna that fell from the heavens when the Israelites wandered in the desert after the Exodus. The manna never fell on the Sabbath or ceremonial holy days. Instead, a 'double portion' would fall the day before the holiday or Sabbath to last for both days.

In some customs, each challah loaf is woven with six strands of dough. Together, the loaves would have a combination of 12 strands, matching the 12 tribes of Israel and the 12 loaves of the showbread offering in the Temple. Other numberings of strands used include three, five and seven. As we shall see later, Jesus' feedings of the 4,000 and the 5,000 are crafted to result in seven and 12 baskets of leftovers respectively.

It is hard to imagine that Caravaggio did not put some considerable effort into his symbolism. The challah bread is a clever exercise of nuance. The supper at Emmaus is not a Sabbath meal. This is, after all, the very first day of Easter, and a Sunday. These two loaves of challah bread being blessed by Caravaggio's Jesus therefore send a new message. Namely, this is a 'double portion' of that eternal bread which has now superseded the manna in the wilderness.

Caravaggio is picturing Jesus in the act of speaking and blessing, just as he does in John 6, following John's account of the feeding of the 5,000. John weaves into this narrative the words of Jesus proclaiming that while Moses gave the Israelites bread, and even though that was manna from heaven, something new has come into being through Jesus. Now, the new and imperishable 'bread from heaven' has come down and is that which gives life to the world. The disciples, awestruck, say, 'Lord, give us this bread', to which Jesus replies, 'I am the bread of life.'

Moreover, Emmaus is the obvious setting for Caravaggio's staged imagery of Jesus, the bread of life, presiding over the challah. The lush and opulent supper is also a cipher rooted in Emmaus itself. A relatively common place name in the Near East, Emmaus literally means the 'spring of salvation' or the 'warm spring', and its name would have meant a town that had a natural spring at source that was invested with healing properties. Here and now it all comes together: bread, water,

wine; the eternal banquet is here, and the first Easter Day proclaims this at the First Supper – after the Last Supper.

You may be forgiven for wondering if the place names of
the Bible, Caravaggio's symbolism and the Gospel referencing
(especially John and Luke) are really present in the Christian
tradition (exegesis) or something we read into the story
(eisegesis). I am not sure this matters greatly. However you
read the Gospels, there is no escaping the interwoven nature
of bread and flesh, water and wine, the Last Supper and the
heavenly banquet. Caravaggio gives us all of this in his *Supper
at Emmaus*.

For Christians, Jesus is the bread of the world. In the Gospels,
Jesus takes bread and shares it: in the feeding of the 4,000, the
5,000, at the Last Supper and in resurrection appearances in
the supper at Emmaus and on the shore of Lake Galilee. In the
New Testament, we are taught we are all one body, for we all
share in one bread. We are taught not to divide the body and
not to be partial about who we feed and nourish: Jesus is for
all and his bread as his body is for all.

The Feast of the Annunciation falls on 25 March – the visit
of the angel Gabriel to Mary to tell her the 'good news' that
she was pregnant and would bear a son – and comes exactly
nine months before Christmas. The immaculate timing of the
annunciation is a proclamation of the immaculate conception
of Jesus and a nine-month gestation. Since medieval times and
indeed long before, the Feast of the Annunciation was called
Lady Day. The Old (or Middle) English meaning of 'Lady' was
'kneader of bread' (*hlafdige*); and a 'Lord' (of the manor or a
shire; *hlafweard*) meant 'keeper of bread'. Even today, vestiges
of the Old English meaning survive: 'dough' is still slang
for money, and we still speak of households having 'bread-
winners'. In Aramaic, Bethlehem meant 'Town of Bread'. In
Arabic, 'Bethlehem' means 'House of Flesh' (or meat). More
colloquially, to be pregnant is to have a 'bun in the oven'.
Indeed, our English word 'bun' comes from an old Gaulish
and Germanic word, meaning swelling or rising. Buns gestate:
just watch the dough rise.

Mary, the mother of Jesus, is the kneader of the dough. It is her 'yes' to God and her gestation that bring forth this utterly unique Fruit of the Spirit, namely the Christ-child, who grows and rises within her and then arises from her. Flesh of our flesh, bone of our bone. The crib in Bethlehem is little more than a large bread basket.

An altar at which the Eucharist is celebrated is a servery – a place from which to give that which was already freely given. So, as we have received this bread freely, this Jesus whom we neither earn nor deserve, so this bread is for all who come to supper at table with that same Jesus who blessed and multiplied the loaves to feed so many thousands, Jews and Gentiles alike.

Mary is therefore both the 'kneader of bread' (*hlafdige*) and a 'Lord' or 'Lady' as the 'keeper of bread' (*hlafweard*). But she keeps it not for herself. She only keeps it to see this single dough rise and become bread for the world. She only keeps, nourishes and cherishes the infant Jesus in order to give him up. He is not hers. He is ours. And because she shares her bread from herself – flesh of her flesh – she is one with us too: the kneader, keeper and the giver of bread.

Readers interested in reflecting further on this theme would be fed and nourished by John Hadley's *Bread of the World: Christ and the Eucharist Today* (1989). The sacramental theology that underwrites the book will not suit all tastes. To my mind, the writings of Richard Holloway and Gerard Hughes SJ are more grounded, though I find Hadley's notion of the Eucharist as 'heaven in ordinary' to be compelling. Jesus is an expression of God's heart for humanity. He is the body language of God. The vision of the kingdom of God (or *kin-dom* of God, as Mujerista theology has it) is in the feasting of this supper. The kin-dom of God is for all. So the ministry of Jesus will incorporate from the outset. It belongs in the alleys, not just the temple. It will welcome Samaritans, not just Sadducees; publicans, not just Pharisees.

Jesus reaches out to the Samaritan woman and tells stories about good Samaritans, much to the annoyance of his potentially loyal Judaean audience. He embraces the widow, the lame, the ostracized, the deprived and despised and the neglected. He befriends the sinners and sinned against. He takes his tea with tax collectors. Jesus heals nobodies; the Gospels, in nearly all cases, are not able to name the afflicted individuals. The people Jesus reached out towards were excluded from the mainstream of society and faith.

What is significant about this? Jesus' kin-dom of God project was, from the outset, supra-tribal. It reached out beyond Judaism to the Gentiles. Indeed, he often praised Gentiles for their faith, and often scolded the apparently 'orthodox' religion of his kith and kin for its insularity and purity. Jesus saw that God was for everyone; he lived, practised and preached this.

We see this in the healing miracles that Jesus wrought – to a Canaanite girl, a Samaritan woman or a Roman centurion's servant. There are crumbs, crusts and loaves for all; to lepers, the blind, the demon-possessed. Jesus touches the untouchable, hears the dumb, speaks to the deaf and sees the blind. His healings are both universal and highly partial, being overwhelmingly directed to the marginalized and ostracized. It is there in parables too, with Jesus constantly teaching us about the least, the last and the lesser. God can't take his loving eyes off the people and situations we most easily neglect.

The ministry of Jesus is startling in its inclusivity. Consider, for example, the feedings of the 5,000 and the 4,000. It is customary, in a kind of lazy-liberal and rather reductive way, to suppose that the Gospel writers simply got their maths muddled and were a bit confused about a single event. But in fact there may be good reasons to regard the two miracles as quite separate. The feeding of the 5,000 takes place on the western banks of the Sea of Galilee. The region was almost entirely Jewish and the 12 baskets of leftovers symbolize the 12 tribes of Israel. Always remember the leftovers: God was thinking about the others who needed to be fed but who could not be here there and then. Jesus' bread keeps for others who cannot make it to this feast. This manna does not go stale.

What then of the feeding of the 4,000 and the seven baskets of leftovers? It takes place, after all, on the same kind of territory as Jesus' healing of the Canaanite girl (the Syrophoenician woman's daughter). The theme of feeding and bread emphasizes that it is shared. The event occurs on the eastern shores of the Sea of Galilee and the region was almost entirely Gentile in composition. Just as we have a healing in Tyre and Sidon, so we have seven baskets of leftovers corresponding to the seven Gentile regions of the time (that is, the territories of Phoenicia, Samaria, Perea, Decapolis, Gaulanitis, Idumea and Philistia).

The parallels are compelling: the baskets in the feeding of the 5,000 (*kophinos*) are smaller than those mentioned in the feeding of the 4,000 (*spuridi* – a basket big enough for a person, as with Paul in Acts 9.25). The point here is that the new manna from heaven will be distributed evenly, across all lands. There is plenty for all. So of course Jesus heals the Canaanite girl – a Gentile, not a Jew. Just as he feeds the 4,000. Matthew and Luke record the same: the feeding of the 4,000 and the healing of the Canaanite girl are linked.

The gospel of Christ is, in other words, radically inclusive: Jew, Greek, Gentile, slave, free – all shall be welcome in the kingdom of God. The Church is meant to be a platform for radical inclusivity. The House of Bread is for sharing. The Church is supposed to be an enduring campaign for the homeless, not a home for campaigners. The good news of the gospel is vested in the accessibility of God: the welcoming in of the religiously marginalized, and the breaking down of barriers. Take another look at Caravaggio's Jesus in the *Supper at Emmaus* and you see something else: hands extended in welcome, blessing the people as they stare back in wonder at this eternal Eucharist.

A Eucharist for the Home

ROBIN GIBBONS

Rubrics for the Eucharist

Have a careful think through where and when this act of worship is to take place, who will be present, and how simplicity can be combined with reverence and mystery. A simple cup, glass or goblet will suffice, with a small plate. Bread and wine sufficient for the numbers present will be all that is needed.

Most of all, remember that in this act of worship, we hold things that connect heaven to earth and humanity to divinity.

The Great Thanksgiving

This is a translation of the prayer of Hippolytus of Rome (c. AD 215) and it is the earliest known text of a Eucharistic Prayer. I use this as a Eucharist for the Home (in a time of confinement or lockdown). To remember the presence of Jesus in your midst, you will need to balance every word with silence. So although this liturgy is very short, you will need:

    bread and wine
    one lit candle
    a simple cup or beaker and a plate
    someone to read the Gospel for the day
    some prayers.

In the name of the Father and of the Son and of the Holy Spirit. Amen.

The Gospel of the day and Prayers of Intercession follow, and a brief silence.

The great thanksgiving

The Lord be with you.
And also with you.

Lift up your hearts.
We lift them up to the Lord.

Let us give thanks to the Lord our God.
It is right to give our thanks and praise.

We give you thanks, O God, through your beloved servant, Jesus Christ, whom you have sent in these last times as saviour and redeemer, and messenger of your will. He is your Word, inseparable from you, through whom you made all things and in whom you take delight.
You sent him from heaven into the Virgin's womb, where he was conceived and took flesh. Born of the Virgin by the power of the Holy Spirit, he was revealed as your Son. In fulfilment of your will he stretched out his hands in suffering to release from suffering those who place their trust in you, and so won for you a holy people.
He freely accepted the death to which he was handed over, in order to destroy death and to shatter the chains of the evil one; to trample underfoot the powers of hell and to lead the righteous into light; to fix the boundaries of death, and to manifest the resurrection.
And so he took bread, gave thanks to you, and said: 'Take, and eat; this is my body, broken for you.' In the same way he took the cup, saying: 'This is my blood, shed for you. When you do this, do it for the remembrance of me.'

Remembering therefore his death and resurrection, we set before you this bread and cup, thankful that you have counted us worthy to stand in your presence and serve you as your priestly people.
We ask you to send your Holy Spirit upon the offering of the holy Church. Gather into one all who share these holy mysteries, filling them with the Holy Spirit and confirming their faith in the truth, that together we may praise you and give you glory, through your servant, Jesus Christ.
Through him all glory and honour are yours, almighty Father, with the Holy Spirit in the holy Church, now and for ever. Amen.

The Lord's Prayer

The Sharing of the bread and wine, with the words: 'the body of Christ' and 'the blood of Christ'.

Prayer after communion

Almighty God, we praise you and thank you that you came for all creation in Jesus. In your Word made flesh, you dwelt among us that all might know your eternal, redeeming love. In this bread and cup that we have received, help us to receive Jesus, our Saviour; to receive your eternal gift for us, so the light that has come into the world might shine in and from our own hearts, and we might join the angels' song: 'Glory to God in the highest and on earth peace, goodwill to all people.' In Jesus' name we pray. Amen.

The Grace

For a Celebration of
Holy Communion

JIM COTTER

This service originally came from Jim Cotter's book The Service of My Love *(Cairns Publications, 2009, pp. 47–53).*

Introduction

The sequence that follows has been used in homes and on pilgrimages, at retreats and on ecumenical occasions. It has no formal authorization. It carries only the authority of the hundreds of people who have contributed to it and worshipped through it. It pays particular attention to bodies, matter and creation, praying for transformation, for transfiguration.

The first few lines of the Prayer of Thanksgiving have their origin in the *Book of Common Prayer of the Episcopal Church in the United States*. The longer of the two invitations to communion was written on Ynys Enlli (Bardsey Island), over-looking the swirling sound between the island and the end of the Lleyn Peninsula. The last two lines of each of the invitations is a quotation from St Augustine.

At the taking of the bread and wine

We bring to this place our living and our dying.
We bring our trust and our doubt.
We bring our friends and our enemies.
We bring the bread that sustains us.
We bring the wine that mellows us.

We bring what has already been changed:
grain and seed,
flour and grape,
baked and pressed,
loaf and vintage.

We bring our substance:
flesh-bodies,
touching and being touched,
life-blood,
circulating and flowing.

We bring our loving:
yearning and broken,
desiring greater intimacy,
longing for greater justice,
knowing that if we do not love one another,
we shall die.

All is gift.
All is grace.
Let us be thankful.
Let us open ourselves to be transformed.

The prayer of thanksgiving

Let us contemplate in wonder, awe, and gratitude
the universe of which we are a part,
the vast expanse of interstellar space,
galaxies, suns, the planets in their courses,
and this beautiful and fragile earth our island home ...

Let us with dignified humility accept our vocation
to be trustees of all that lives and breathes under the sun,
to be skilful in probing the mysteries of creation,
to be wise and reverent in our use of the resources of
	the earth ...

So let us greet the God who is within us and beyond us:

Creator Spirit, Energy Inspiring,
brooding over the formless deeps,
wings outstretched in the primal dark,
enclosing and calling forth all that has come to be,
ever present to renew and re-create ...
beckoning all that is chaotic and without form –
the spontaneous leap of microscopic particles,
the isolated impulse of the human heart –
weaving them into the pattern of a larger whole ...

urging forward into ever more complex forms of life ...

planting an awareness and faint yearning for
	the unattained ...
challenging a choosing of the unknown yet to be,
a risk that is a dying that a fuller life be born,
a sacrifice of lesser ways, a giving up of slaughter,
the law of gentleness in the midst of force and fury ...

a way made known to us by Jesus of Nazareth,
eternal persuasive love made visible at last ...

the love that through the aeons of unrecorded time
    has striven and suffered, died and risen to new life,
within the very fabric of the universe,
accepting us so deeply that we need no longer seize and possess
    out of malice and of fear,
clearing the way for us to be empowered
    to mend creation's threads that we have torn,
to make the desert bloom
    and the trees to grow again on barren ground ...

So we take the produce of this earth,
the bread of our sustenance,
the wine of our solace and our sorrow,
    as Jesus commanded us to do,
that we might know Creator Spirit
    transfiguring our flesh and blood
    to a glory that we but dimly sense,
filling us with the living presence,
the very self, of Jesus,
given, sacrificed for us,
to bring us alive,
to bring us together as one body.

For he took bread, gave thanks, broke it,
and gave it to his disciples and said,

Take, eat, this is my Body
which is given for you:
do this to re-member me.

In the same way, after supper,
he took a cup of wine, gave thanks,
and gave it to them and said,

Drink of this, all of you,
this is my Blood of the new covenant,
which is shed for you and for many
for the forgiveness of sins:

do this, as often as you drink it,
to re-member me.

Creator Spirit, as we celebrate the one great sacrifice of love,
hover now over your people,
over this bread and wine,
that they may be to us the
Body and Blood of Christ.

For in the mystery of faith,

Christ has died,
Christ is risen,
Christ is here,
Christ will come.

And now with all who have ever lived,
with saints and martyrs and forgotten faithful people,
with angels and archangels and all the heavenly company,
with all who are alive and all who are yet to be born,
with all creation in all time, with joy we sing:

(This verse can be sung to the tune Nicaea)

Holy! Holy! Holy! Beating heart of glory!
All your works shall praise your Name in earth and sky
and sea!
Holy! Holy! Holy! Strong in Love and Mercy!
Living Communion, Blessed Trinity!

Blessed is the One who comes in the Name of our God:
Hosanna in the Highest!

Alleluia! Praise to the God of Splendour!
So be it! Amen!

The breaking of the bread

The bread which we break
is a sharing in the Body of Christ.

The wine which we bless
is a sharing in the Blood of Christ.

Body and Blood of one humanity,
we shall be transfigured to glory.

We break this bread for all the peoples of faith,
so often divided by hatred and suspicion –

we break this bread for the earth and oceans,
plundered and torn by human hands –

we break this bread for the destitute and starving,
the grieving and the stigmatized,
and for all the broken-hearted –

we break this bread for the wounded child within each one
of us.

The invitation to communion

Either:
Let us open our hands,
open our hearts,
open the hidden places of our being,
and into our deep soul-self
let them enter the heartbeat of those we love,
the lifeblood of our villages, towns, and cities,
the life stream of the tides and currents and seasons,
the pulsing of our planet and of the stars;
let them enter all the joys and pains our cup can bear;
let us be nourished by the new life
that comes through what is broken;
and in and through it all,

to transform it to glory,
let us receive the Body, the Living Presence,
the Blood, the Very Self, of Jesus,
and let us feed and live and love,
in faith, with gratitude.

Beloved, we draw near to be loved by you,
in deep yet trembling trust,
through this matter of your creation,
this material stuff of bread and body,
this fluid of wine and blood,
that your desire for us and ours for you
may be blended in deep joy and ecstasy,
that we may be enriched and doubly blessed.

**We draw near to receive this offering of yourself,
your intimate, vulnerable, and naked body,
imparted to us, incorporated in us,
that we may dwell and love and create,
you in us and we in you.**

Receive who you are.
Become what you see.

Or:
The bread of life,
love embodied,
nourish you.

The life-blood,
love expended,
enliven you.

Feed on the Living One,
full of humanity,
laced with divinity.

Feed on the Loving One,
by faith,
with thanksgiving.

Receive who you are.
Become what you see.

A final blessing

The blessing of God be with us,
Father and Mother,
Sustainer of our earth,
Source of all that is and that shall be.

The blessing of God be with us,
the universal Christ,
the Risen and Glorious Loved One,
and our Friend.

The blessing of God be with us,
Spirit spreading love and joy in our hearts,
giving hope to the battered ones,
inspiring justice and peace for the little ones.

**May this rich blessing be with us,
with all humankind living and departed,
and with all the creatures
of land and sea and air.
May our days be long on this good earth.**

**For we have been nourished
by the Bread of Life,
we have been quickened
by the Life-blood of the Universe.
With courage and hope
let us continue on the journey.
Amen. Thanks be to God.**

Shorter Eucharist

This is a South African Liturgy, devised by the Church of the Holy Family, Blackbird Leys, Oxford, for children preparing for confirmation, where we invite them to ask questions in a similar way to the Shabbat.

The Lord be with you.
And also with you.
Lift up your hearts.
We lift them to the Lord.
Let us give thanks to the Lord our God.
It is right to give him thanks and praise.

As we give thanks, we ask …
Why do we give thanks and praise at this table?
We give thanks for all that God has done for us. God the
Father created the heavens, the earth and everything in them;
and created us in his own image, and has given us life. He is
the reason behind everything, and yet loves each and every
one of us.

God sent the Holy Spirit to gather us together as the people
   of God.
So come, let us join together to worship this God who
   loves us.
Holy, Holy, Holy Lord, God of power and might.
Heaven and earth are full of your glory,
hosanna in the highest.
Blessed is he who comes in the name of the Lord.
Hosanna in the highest.

We praise you, Father, that before Jesus our Saviour died, he gave us this holy meal.

Why do we eat bread together at this table?

On the night before he died, Jesus took bread. After giving thanks he broke it, and gave it to the disciples saying, 'Take, eat. This is my body given for you. Do this in remembrance of me.' Here we remember that Jesus becomes present here and he feeds us as we share in him with others around this holy altar. From one bread we all become united as his children.

Why do we drink from the cup together at this table?

In the same way, after supper Jesus took the cup, saying, 'This cup is God's new covenant sealed with my blood, poured out for you for the forgiveness of sins. Do this in remembrance of me.' This is a sign of Jesus' saving love, poured out for us when he died on the cross.

What do we remember at this table?

We remember the Father's gracious love for us, Christ's death and resurrection for us, and the Spirit's tender care for us. Let us proclaim the mystery of faith.

Christ has died,
Christ is risen,
Christ will come again.

Merciful Father, pour out your Holy Spirit on us and on these gifts of bread and wine. In eating and drinking together, may we be made one with Christ and with one another. **Amen.**

As our Saviour taught us, we say together,

Our Father who art in heaven, hallowed be thy name.
Thy kingdom come. Thy will be done on earth, as it is
in heaven.
Give us this day our daily bread.
Forgive us our trespasses, as we forgive those who trespass
against us.
Lead us not into temptation, but deliver us from evil: For
thine is the kingdom, the power, and the glory, for ever and
ever. Amen.

Draw near with faith, receive the body of our Lord Jesus Christ
which he gave for you and his blood which he shed for you.
Eat and drink in remembrance that he died for you
and feed on him in your hearts by faith and with thanksgiving.

After communion

Let us pray.
Author of Salvation, you have written us into the book of
life. You have written us into your story. Help us to continue
your work of love, forgiveness and reconciliation, so that we
might tell your story to those who have not heard, that we
might include those who have felt rejected. Help us to read
the threads woven into your story that we have not seen or
heard – stories of those who are different from us in culture
and practice, those who speak different languages, those who
have different families and abilities. Help us to learn and grow
and to live out your story of love for all. In your name, Jesus,
we pray. Amen.

'A Fragrant Offering and Sacrifice'

2 Corinthians 4.7–15; Mark 6.14–29
(A Eucharist for Martyrs, Charterhouse Chapel,
September 2016)

MARTYN PERCY

Immortalization is a funny business. 'It's not easy to represent theological ideas by using taste buds alone,' Blaise Poyet told a press conference in Geneva, 'so the Federation of Swiss Protestant Churches set me an interesting challenge. For me, Jean Calvin was just a reformer I learned about long ago at school, but when I was asked to capture his essence in chocolate form, I could not resist. The key thing for Calvin was the glory of God, his excellence, his perfection. So naturally, I chose a chocolate that is exceptional, rare, and flawless.'

Poyet, a master chocolatier from Vevey, was unveiling his new Calvin bon-bons (priced at £11.50 per dozen), ahead of the 500th anniversary of the Protestant Reformer's birth in 2009:

The first layer is based on a classic smooth and runny praline mix. 'But we have "reformed" it,' says the Vevey chocolatier, by using crunchy caramelised hazelnuts, and using salt from the Swiss Alps to make the praline slightly savoury.

The second layer uses a 'chocolate Grand Cru from Bolivia', made from 68 percent cocoa paste, to represent Calvin's theology of the glory and perfection of God.

'It is a real pleasure,' Poyet says of the Bolivian chocolate. 'Paradise indeed.'

Some historians have noted Calvin was not always an easy person, yet 'it is undeniable that in his actions, he demonstrated exceptional tenderness,' recounts Poyet. 'So we have used a caramel made from Swiss cream that slightly softens the chocolate to represent in a discreet way this love for one's neighbour.'

Finally, a taste of lemon verbena, a perennial, represents Calvin's ability to sow, to plant and to make things grow.[1]

Just so I can head your minds off at the pass, you will be aware that your average Oxford College fellowship is immortalized in chocolate. After all, to what else can 'Quality Street' possibly refer? Although some of you will be sitting there thinking – surely he means 'Assorted Fudge'? But my point is a serious one. Christianity is a faith of the senses. We often think of texts to read; sights to see; words to hear. But we seldom think of our faith as something to taste – and even smell – which is peculiar, because Christian faith is one that is redolent with meaning when it engages all our senses. Consider this account, for example, of the death of Polycarp from the early *Acts of the Christian Martyrs* (AD 155):

> [T]he men in charge of the fire started to light it. A great flame blazed up and those of us to whom it was given to see beheld a miracle ... for the flames, bellying out like a ship's sail in the wind, formed into the shape of a vault and thus surrounded the martyr's body as with a wall. And he was within it not as burning flesh, but rather as bread being baked, or like gold and silver being purified in a smelting furnace. And from it we perceived such a delightful fragrance as though it were smoking incense or some other costly perfume.[2]

Christianity is a faith of the senses. There are things of beauty to see and texts to read; sounds and words to hear; artefacts and objects to touch; and sacraments to taste and savour. But we rarely think of our faith in terms of its sense of smell. This is all rather surprising when one considers just how important the olfactory imagination is in the ancient world: the scent of salvation, to borrow a phrase from one theologian (Susan Ashbrook Harvey). For in the scents, smells and odours of Scripture, tradition and Church, we have intimations of the divine. As one anthropologist, Clifford Geertz, says, 'religious symbols *reek* of meaning'. And sometimes they literally do reek – the message is in the scent.

In the account of the martyrdom of Polycarp, we are introduced to the resonances between scent and meaning: the aroma of baking bread is a eucharistic hint, and the smell of gold or silver being purified a promise for believers. Here, in Polycarp's death, we have the hint of salvation and eternal life for all believers. The early Christians were also keenly in touch with the senses of smell and taste, and their links with worship and the presence of God. Christ is both bread and wine; to taste and see is to enter into communion. This is not just cerebral; it is also sensual. Manna in the wilderness, or sweet water in the desert, are tokens of both comfort and abiding nourishment. Ephesians 5.2 tells us 'to live in love, as Christ loved us and gave himself for us, a fragrant offering and sacrifice to God'. In 2 Corinthians, Paul writes: 'But thanks be to God, who in Christ leads us in triumphal procession, and through us spreads in every place the *fragrance* that comes from knowing him' (2.14–16).

The Carthusian martyrs of London were the monks of Charterhouse, the monastery of the Carthusian Order in central London, and were put to death by the English state in a period lasting from 4 May 1535 until 20 September 1537. The method of execution was hanging, disembowelling while still alive and then quartering. The group also included two monks who were brought from the Charterhouses of Beauvale and Axholme and similarly dealt with. The death toll was 18 men, all of whom have been recognized as true martyrs.

But a question: why these methods of death? What is it about this kind of killing or execution that we find so dreadful? Well, first a word about terror. As the literal meaning of the word indicates, 'terror' is a military strategy that hopes to change the political situation by spreading fear rather than by causing enormous material damage. Every military action spreads fear. But in conventional warfare, fear is a *by-product* of material losses. In terrorism or dictatorship, fear is the whole story and there is an astounding disproportion between the actual strength of the terrorists or dictators and the fear they manage to inspire.

Second, there is also something symbolic about hanging, beheading, disembowelling and quartering. This is about dis-membering. We know from Scripture that faces – our face and the face of God – are how we are known, recognized and ultimately cherished. To remove the head is to remove a person's identity – to literally erase someone. And that word – erase – means, literally, 'to scrape off, shave; abolish, remove'. A hanging throttles the voice; a beheading cuts through the neck and the throat, terminating the breath and speech; it renders the mouth apart from the body. The neck is one of the most vulnerable parts of the human body. Rendered asunder, no feeding and no breathing means there will be no more life. This person will not speak again; erased, their body now becomes anonymous – a mere nothing.

Third, you can begin to see why, perhaps, the beheadings are not just part of terrorism – whether by groups or by movements – but also part of a nation's or state's weaponry. In Nanjing, China, at the Museum of the Holocaust, the Chinese people commemorate the thousands of their citizens dismembered by the conquering Japanese forces in World War Two. The Nazis executed thousands of prisoners by beheading. Perhaps surprisingly, France only banned beheading in 1981 – under François Mitterrand. It was the only legal means of capital punishment in France from 1789 until the end of the twentieth century.

Beheading, then, even in the hands of the state, is vindictive; it is a statement of triumph; of total victory; of annihilation. It is the destruction and humiliation of a body. (One former resident of the Deanery at Christ Church, Oxford, met his death this way – Charles I.)

And so we come to the last verse of our Gospel: '[John's disciples] came and took his body, and laid it in a tomb' (Mark 6.29). No further explanation is needed. There will be no retribution. Like Jesus on the cross, this unjust violence and death is absorbed, and not returned. Instead, there is real tenderness, kindness and wisdom in the face of loss. You see the shadows of this, even in a schmaltzy film such as *Love Actually* (2003), where Hugh Grant opens with these words:

> General opinion's starting to make out that we live in a world of hatred and greed, but I don't see that ... When the planes hit the Twin Towers, as far as I know none of the phone calls from the people on board were messages of hate or revenge – they were all messages of love.

Martyrs live in love and die in love, so they are quite different from suicide bombers. Suicide bombers plant seeds of hate. But martyrs, even in death, grow only love. They fulfil what Jesus proclaims in John 12.24 – which might as well be about the Carthusians: 'Very truly, I tell you, unless a grain of wheat falls into the earth and dies, it remains just a single grain; but if it dies, it bears much fruit.'

That is why Tertullian (150–240) can say, 100 years after John wrote his Gospel, that 'the blood of the martyrs is the seed of the Church'. Or, as Paul would have it, they are the treasures of the Church, in our earthenware pots. We carry the death of Jesus in our bodies, so God's life may be manifest in us. We are given over to death for Jesus' sake, so that the life of Jesus may be manifested in our mortal flesh.

John the Baptist's disciples simply came and collected his body, and carried on with the business of love and faith. The response to the death of their beloved leader was not a hateful revenge but rather faithfulness and love. And so where does this place John the Baptist? Or for that matter, some irritant rebellious Carthusian monks? They move in life, and especially in death, from being regional political and religious irritants, to being true 'catholic' martyrs. 'He must increase, I must decrease' is John the Baptist's prayer (John 3.30). Martyrs live in love and die in love. And so we commemorate 18 Carthusians who, though dead, loved to the end – and so continue to live in our hearts and histories. Enduring love is their legacy.

Notes

1 See Stephen Brown, 'Chocolate tribute highlight's Calvin's sweet side', https://old.ekklesia.co.uk/node/7921 (accessed 15.11.2022).

2 Susan Ashbrook Harvey, *Scenting Salvation: Ancient Christianity and the Olfactory Imagination*, Berkeley, CA: University of California Press, 2006, p. 7.

BIRTH AND BAPTISM

Birth is where we all begin. Baptism, where we begin again. It is not that God paid no regard to our first beginning. We are known and loved as we come to full term, having been knit together. The ancient rabbis thought that life began with the first breath a baby took, just as God's creation and the Holy Spirit is imparted with breath. The life breathed into the first humans mirrors the final act of Jesus breathing on the disciples in the Gospel of John, so they receive the Holy Spirit. Baptism, likewise, is the act of cleansing and renewal. All known life on our planet requires water. In these liturgies, poems, prayers and homilies, we explore that water of life that flows abundantly from Christ.

Have a careful think through where and when this act of worship is to take place, who will be present, and how simplicity can be combined with reverence and mystery. Sometimes a simple bowl, jug and towel will be all that is needed. But most of all, remember that in this act of worship we hold things that connect heaven to earth and humanity to divinity.

A Simple Service of Baptism

CHURCH OF THE HOLY FAMILY,
BLACKBIRD LEYS, OXFORD

This short ecumenical Service of Baptism is intended to be inclusive and accessible. The text offers material for the beginning and ending of the baptism, and also prayers to supplement the essential symbols in baptism – the water, cross and candle. We follow the simple proverb in liturgy: Less is More. Let the symbols, actions and the presence of the Holy Spirit in the gathering do their work in the baptizing.

The **water of baptism** is

- a symbol of our new birth into life with Christ;
- a visible sign of God's love pouring down upon the person being baptized;
- a visible sign of God's forgiveness, renewing them and transforming the mistakes they have made (or will make) into something new and creative – like water gradually smoothing jagged stones.

The **sign of the cross** made with the oil of baptism is

- a symbol that the person being baptized belongs to God;
- a symbol that they live and grow as a follower of Christ;
- a symbol of the Holy Spirit guiding and strengthening them day by day.

The **lighted candle** is

- a reminder that Jesus is the Light of the World who passed through the darkness of death to the light of resurrection;
- a reminder that God's light overcomes every darkness;
- a reminder that God's love and light shine out of the person being baptized among their families and friends and into the world.

Call to worship

Leader: The Lord has examined me and he knows me.
People: **The Lord knows everything I do, and he understands all my thoughts.**
Leader: The Lord's knowledge of me is too deep.
People: **It is beyond my understanding.**
Leader: Come, let us worship God who has complete knowledge of us.

Opening hymn

All things bright and beautiful; He's got the whole world in his hands; Morning has broken; Lord of the Dance (it is advisable to choose well-known hymns)

Prayer

If God is in every person we meet, what does that say about the harmful words we speak, the hurt we cause to others in our lives? We are invited to bring our faults and foolishness, our brokenness and bitterness to our God, confessing them, so we might be made new.

You know us. You know who we are, we find it easier to hold on to all we do that is wrong. You know what we do, when we ignore the poor or refuse to live at peace with others. You know why we do all these things. You do indeed know

us all too well. Yet, you continue to be patient with us and forgiving towards us. You embrace us as we turn towards you in regret. You continue to call us to follow Jesus Christ, our Lord and Saviour, so we might find our life with you.

Listen to God's voice: I walk with you in every moment; I fill you with grace and hope; I know you and love you. Amen.

Reading

Suggested readings: Psalm 46.10; Psalm 62.1; Psalm 65.1; Isaiah 30.15; Zephaniah 1.7; Lamentations 3.26; Mark 1.35; Revelation 8.1; 1 Kings 19.11–12

Sermon following the act of baptism

We rejoice with them, with their families and with their friends. We pray that their lives will be happy and filled with the great things that God has promised to his children. May they walk tall and proud as children of the living God.
Alleluia!

We have remembered that we too have been chosen and welcomed into the community of faith.

We renew our faith and go on our way to live, to love and to tell the good news – that Jesus Christ is Lord!
Alleluia!

Blessing

May the transforming love of God work in your lives, today and always. Go forth into the world with peace, love and joy. Follow Christ wherever he leads you. Fulfil the promise found in the fruit of the Spirit.
And the blessing of God almighty, Father, Son and Holy Spirit, be with you and remain with you this day and always.
Amen.

The Nature and Nurture of Jesus

Exodus 2.1–10; Colossians 3.12–17; John 19.25–27

MARTYN PERCY

Mary and Joseph both take a risk: 'Mary said to the angel, "How can this be, since I am a virgin?"' (Luke 1.34). But by accepting something alien, rejection is avoided and hospitality and love are shown instead. Hospitality, love and redemption are, in turn, bestowed on humanity through God in Christ.

The Scriptures feed us well, but it doesn't mean everything we eat is easy to digest. Sometimes you have to engage with the powerful emotions behind the stories we know so well. Sarah, Abraham's wife, never speaks again after the proposed sacrifice of Isaac. Scripture innocently records her deathly silence. But what would you say to your husband who had just taken your son on a long trip, bound and gagged him, raised a knife to offer him to God, only to be stopped – the voice of God halting him mid-sacrifice in the middle of the liturgy, I mean is nothing sacred?! – and then returned home. That must have been an interesting conversation over the breakfast table the next day.

Perhaps you may know the 'Cherry Tree Carol', a ballad reportedly sung in some form at the Feast of Corpus Christi in the early fifteenth century. The ballad relates an apocryphal story of the Virgin Mary, presumably while travelling to Bethlehem with Joseph for the census. In the most popular version, the two stop in a cherry orchard and Mary asks her husband to pick cherries for her, citing her child within. Joseph

– cuckolded by the Holy Spirit, let us remember – spitefully tells Mary to let the child's father pick her own cherries. At this point in most versions, the infant Jesus, from the womb, speaks to the tree and commands it to lower a branch down to Mary, which it does. Joseph, witnessing this miracle, immediately repents of his harsh words.

Now, I am not asking you to go away and read Pseudo-Matthew from the New Testament Apocrypha, from which this story comes. The cherry tree story is merely an invitation to put yourself in Joseph's shoes. He is, in Christian orthodoxy, the stepfather of Jesus, loving a child he may not have wanted and did not plan, but whom he must raise as his own.

I began life unplanned and unwanted. A second child, born out of wedlock and to a mother who would have four children in all – and all by different men. She kept numbers one and four and gave away numbers two and three. My birth father was married too, and I am the middle child of his three. His wife (deceased) and two sons had no idea of his extra-marital affair and the resulting child. I am a Livingstone on his side and a Rowlands on hers. So, bizarrely, a distant relative of both David Livingstone, the missionary explorer, and Henry Morton Stanley, the *Times* reporter who found him in Africa. But Stanley was not his real name. He had changed it after the American Civil War, dropping his birth name, Rowlands, for the more distinguished confederate captain he had served, but who had died in combat. My birth name was David. So yes, I could have been Dr David Livingstone; and also related to the *Times* reporter who asks, 'Dr Livingstone, I presume?'

I was born in 1962 in what used to be called 'a home for naughty girls', in Blackburn, Lancashire – far away from the curtain-twitching neighbours of my birth mother's street in south Manchester. It was a bad birth; and for about a year, the doctors thought I might be physically damaged and with learning difficulties. (I realize some of you are thinking, crumbs, that was a good early spot by the doctors.) But I was formally adopted before I was a year old and immediately baptized at St Frideswyde's church, near Liverpool. I only mention this because Frideswyde is the patron saint of the city, university and diocese of Oxford, and when I visited her shrine a few years ago, I had what I can only describe as an epiphany; almost another kind of baptism in the Spirit. And I realized I was now inside a kind of true 'mother church' – St Frideswyde's own – and I was home, in a strange yet very real sense.

Now, a change of tack, if you will. If you think about it, there is a lot of bad parenting in the Bible. And some good parenting too. There is a lot of good adoption, by the way; and some not so good. Quite a lot of children and parents change their names. Siblings squabble and even murder; it's complex, isn't it? So the theologian Elizabeth Stuart urges caution when people appeal for a return to 'biblical family values'. 'Which ones?' she asks. She points out that there are at least 42 models in the Old Testament, and you won't want to practise some of them. For example, after years of childlessness, Sarah urges her husband Abraham to conceive a child with her slave, Hagar (Genesis 16). Though brief, this episode describes a practice of surrogacy, in which a female slave of a childless, higher-status woman bears a child to the woman's husband. She does this by giving birth squatting underneath Sarah. Not an easy family situation to explain to your bishop, perhaps. A return to biblical family values? *Cave Quid Optes*: be careful what you wish for!

It is an age when many people are interested in their ancestors, and in researching them. But if I am honest, I am much more interested in my descendants. Some people are interested in their families for snobbish reasons or for pride. Other people are ashamed of their parental or family background; and many suffer from the knowledge of illegitimacy, adoption or other backgrounds. But in any of these extremes, Jesus speaks to us. So many of us come from unusual backgrounds of which we may be ashamed. Yet in his birth at Bethlehem, Jesus was like us in every respect, including his family circumstances! He had some good and some bad ancestors. Michael Goulder's 1965 poem, entitled 'Tamar', puts it well:

Tamar

Exceedingly odd,
Is the means by which God
Has provided our path to the heavenly shore:
Of the girls from whose line
The true light was to shine
There was one an adulteress, one was a whore.
There was Tamar who bore –
What we all should deplore –
A fine pair of twins to her father-in-law;
And Rahab the harlot,
Her sins were as scarlet,
As red as the thread which she hung from the door;
Yet alone of her nation
She came to salvation,
And lived to be mother of Boaz of yore;
And he married Ruth,
A Gentile uncouth,
In a manner quite counter to biblical law;
And of her there did spring
Blessed David the King
Who walked on his palace one evening,
And saw
The wife of Uriah,
From whom he did sire
A baby that died, oh, and princes a score.
And a mother unmarried
It was too that carried
God's son, and him laid in a cradle of straw;
That the moral might wait
At the heavenly gate
While the sinners and publicans go in before,
Who have not earned their place
But received it by grace,
And have found them a righteousness not of the law.[1]

Four women. All ancestors of Jesus. All with dodgy back-grounds. Either moral failures or born in the wrong place. And Jesus came from people like that. About 400 years ago, the Revd Thomas Fuller (1608–61), an Anglican priest, focused on the fathers in Jesus' genealogy, in another poem:

> Lord, I find the genealogy of my Saviour strangely chequered, with four remarkable changes in four generations.
>
> Rehoboam begat Abijah: (A bad father begat a bad son)
> Abijah begat Asa: (A bad father and a good son)
> Asa begat Jehoshaphat: (A good father and a good son)
> Jehoshaphat begat Jehorom: (A good father and a bad son).
> I see Lord, from hence,
> That my Father's piety cannot be handed on:
> That is bad news for me.
> I see also that actual impiety is not hereditary,
> That is good news for my son!

Why does all this matter? Well, God has many children. But God has no grandchildren. You can't pass your faith down the family line – try as you might. Righteousness is not inherited. We work to bring his kingdom to individuals in the here and now.

We all have to be adopted by God. That's why our mother-ing matters so much. Our faith is not gained by descent but by nurture. So the link between the Exodus story and the end of John's Gospel is, quite literally, adoption. Mothering those who are not yours; not just your own. Caring for those out-side your family; not just those on the inside. Be a mother to the motherless; a father to the fatherless. You can now see the point of the Colossians reading and its stress on virtues. It is about the here and now.

And – thinking especially of those preparing for ministry in the Church – remember the example of Jesus as a pattern for your ministry. John's Gospel tells us that Jesus 'made his home amongst us'; he dwelt 'with us'. He is Emmanuel. Now he wants us to do this for others. It is easy, in ministry, to run an orderly house of God. But that is not the challenge. The challenge is, how do you make the house of God a home for others? Because God invites us home. That's why Jesus made his home among us; so we might be at home with him. There is a world of difference between a house and a home.

The disciple John adopts the mother of Jesus, just as she, in some way, had to struggle with Joseph to accept Jesus. We must make room for the alien, the stranger, the orphan and the other ... and realize they are God's gift to us. We read from Matthew 1.18–25:

Now the birth of Jesus the Messiah took place in this way. When his mother Mary had been engaged to Joseph, but before they lived together, she was found to be with child from the Holy Spirit. Her husband Joseph, being a righteous man and unwilling to expose her to public disgrace, planned to dismiss her quietly. But just when he had resolved to do this, an angel of the Lord appeared to him in a dream and said, 'Joseph, son of David, do not be afraid to take Mary as your wife, for the child conceived in her is from the Holy Spirit. She will bear a son, and you are to name him Jesus, for he will save his people from their sins.' All this took place to fulfil what had been spoken by the Lord through the prophet:
  'Look, the virgin shall conceive and bear a son,
    and they shall name him Emmanuel',
which means, 'God is with us.' When Joseph awoke from sleep, he did as the angel of the Lord commanded him; he took her as his wife, but had no marital relations with her until she had borne a son; and he named him Jesus.

Notes

1 Michael Goulder, *Midrash and Lection*, London: SPCK, 1974, p. 232.

Does the Bible Really Advocate the Nuclear Family?

MARTYN PERCY

Agrapha is not a word in common use. But it usually refers to sayings attributed to Jesus in other parts of the New Testament, but which we don't find in the Gospels. There are not many of them, but one of the best examples comes from Acts 20.35: '[Remember] the words of the Lord Jesus, for he himself said: "It is more blessed to give than to receive."' Jesus might have said this but the Gospels don't record that. However, we know that Plato and Aristotle said similar things, centuries before. Then there is *pseudepigrapha* – things Jesus and the Scriptures never said but people think are in the Bible anyway, such as 'God helps those who help themselves.'

So what of 'nuclear family'? It sounds biblical, doesn't it? I mean, the way that so many in the Church talk about it being sacred and fundamental to society and the foundation of Christendom, you could be forgiven for thinking that Christianity was right behind the nuclear family. But I beg to differ. Jesus advocated leaving one's parents for the sake of the kingdom. His siblings, too, got some short shrift from Jesus. He told his disciples to go and do likewise, more or less. Moreover, don't even think about loitering at your parents' funerals; there is kingdom work to be done. The dead can bury the dead.

The Bible contains many patterns of family life. Some include slaves, such as Hagar, with Abraham and Sarah. In Genesis 16, we read that Hagar becomes a surrogate mother to raise a child for the couple. Family dynamics are complicated at the best of times, but the Old Testament offers us dozens – literally – of 'family patterns', which should not necessarily be honoured today.

For example, few Christians would condone the family dynamics set out in Genesis 29—30, in which Rachel obligingly lends Bilhah (who is Rachel's slave or handmaid) to Jacob so that they can have a son. Rachel says this: 'Here is my maid Bilhah; go in to her, that she may bear children upon my knees and that I too may have children through her' (Genesis 30.3). So even the birth of their son (he is named Dan) is an intimate three-way affair.

Rachel's sister, Leah, when she later realizes she cannot have children either, follows suit and lends her woman servant Zilpah to Jacob too, such is their sibling rivalry. Under this biblical family pattern, Jacob is sleeping with at least four women at any one time, and all under the approving eye of Rachel and Leah's father, Laban, who offers both his daughters to Jacob (Genesis 29).

It should come as no surprise to most people that the word 'nuclear' is not in the Bible. But it comes as a much greater surprise to the same number that 'family' is not really a biblical term either – if by that, we mean husband, wife and 2.4 children. The families that Jesus knew in his day were, on the whole, rather more extended affairs. They were 'households' (*oikos* is the Greek word that the New Testament uses), and they were extensive not intensive; externalized rather than internalized. Can you explain what is meant by these terms?

More on this in a moment, but to set this in context, a question for starters. Was Jesus a good person because of his nature or due to his nurture? A tutorial question I sometimes used to set for undergraduates was to spot the connection between Moses, the Buddha, Muhammad and Jesus. True, they are all great religious leaders. And yes, they all founded major world religions.

But there is also something stranger that connects them. They are all adopted. Moses was abandoned by his birth mother and left to float in a small coracle in the River Nile and had the good fortune to be picked up by the daughter of one of the Pharaohs, and nurtured as one of her own. Muhammad was orphaned at the age of six, or perhaps earlier, and was brought up by his uncle in the ancient city of Makka. The Buddha's mother died when he was less than a week old, and he was raised by her sister. Jesus, of course, according to Christian orthodoxy, is not exactly the child of Joseph, since Christian tradition claims no human intervention in his genesis. Although Mary is clearly his mother, Joseph is not his biological father.

As for the nature–nurture equation, one has to remember that the early church was not a new kind of eclectic synagogue; or for that matter, another recent addition to the long list of temple cults that were available. Rather, the early church chose to base itself on the model of another venerable institution: the *oikos* or 'household'. This formed the nucleus of what we now call 'church'.

Now, an *oikos* was not the cosy insular home like today's ideal 'nuclear family'. An *oikos* was something else – an extended household incorporating kith and kin, servants, slaves, tutors, workers, dependants and contributors. It was an outward-facing and inclusive body that took to adoption quite naturally. It understood that just as God had adopted us, so we, in turn, were to adopt others. And as God had abided with us, so were we to abide with others. Jesus, as ever, modelled not just church but society.

So in the early church, we find Jews, Greeks and Romans; slave and free; male and female. All are one in Christ. In these new assemblies of believers, all were equal. Today, churches rarely think about their identity in self-conscious ways. They mostly go about their business assuming their values and implicitly imbibing these from one generation to the next. But we might pause and reflect here on the ways in which the Church acts as a proto-typical adoptive agency within society. Thus, welcoming the strangers and aliens in their midst, and not only giving to them but also receiving from them.

One key to understanding this, in ecclesial terms, is to see that the dynamic of adoption is one of those implicit values that lie at the heart of the Church and healthy society. That is to say, just as churches, congregations and individual Christians understand or experience themselves as, in some sense, 'adopted' by God (as Paul suggests), so they in turn find themselves adopting others. And the facets of adoption, though plentiful in ecclesial life, remain largely implicit in churches, embedded in everyday acts of charity and hospitality, yet rarely reflected upon.

When most people think about adoption, it is a habit of the heart to believe that it is the child who has somehow, as I have said, been rescued, and that the adopted parents are the redeemers. However, one of the extraordinary things about the majority of the world's great religions is that this equation is turned around – as most things are in religion – so that the adopted child becomes the redeemer, or the gift. This is particularly true in Christian thinking where orthodoxy teaches a kind of double adoption: in return for God's adoption of us by Jesus, we are ourselves adopted into the life of God. Moreover, the adoption is invariably what I would call a 'cross-border risk', where one party takes on something alien, and both redeems it through hospitality and love, and in so doing is redeemed.

But to find this out, our churches and contemporary society have to be prepared to take profound risks in adoption. No matter what our social echelon or ecclesial tradition, there is something about the giving–receiving axis in major religious traditions, and their founders viewed (even just metaphorically) as adoptees – Moses, Buddha, Muhammad and Jesus – that invites churches and societies to reflect on the nature of their composition and hospitality. Moreover, in transcending our normal boundaries and comfort zones, we can find love and perhaps the trace of a more inclusive society. Somewhere, deep in this dynamic, the Church and society discover reciprocity through hospitality: it is in giving that we receive.

Churches, I think, know this – at least at an implicit level. Go to almost any church or congregation on any Sunday and you'll find folk who bond together pretty well, often because of an explicit homogeneity – class, ethnicity or some other socio-cultural factor. Sometimes the explicitness is even a matter of doctrinal bonding. But take a closer look, and what do you find?

Invariably one also sees strangers in the midst of such bodies. Those who know they belong, somehow, but simply don't correspond to the homogeneity of the group; and there are those who simply don't fit in – anywhere. Those same people are often cherished (or at the very least tolerated) by that same congregation and church, and also bring that body gifts; and also point to a strange diversity that is beyond ordinary comprehension. Here we find the implicit spirit of adoption at work.

To some extent, it is a pity that the term 'inclusive' today has become so bound up with a slightly tribal and 'liberal' identity. But perhaps this should not surprise us. For the word 'include' began its life with a fairly insular definition. Drawing from the Latin word *includere*, it means to 'to shut in, enclose or imprison' – just as 'exclude' meant to 'shut out'. But Jesus is not for either option. The defining character of the kingdom of God Jesus inaugurated draws from a rather richer word: *incorporate*. That is to say, to put something into the body or substance of something else; from the Latin *incorporare*, it means to 'unite into one body'.

The kingdom of God, like the Church, was to be one of hybridity. And this is a social vision, not just an ecclesial template. The lesson Jesus learnt in his childhood, and embodied in adulthood, is this. God brings us all together. He's all done with working through a single tribe or race. The Church that begins at Pentecost has been dress-rehearsed in Jesus' ministry: it will be multi-lingual, multi-cultural and multi-racial. It will be multiple. We, though being many, are one body.

Christians, it is often said, believe in unity but not uniformity. It is the spirit of adoption that underpins this dynamic. The eventual and explicit surfacing of diversity is caused by the implicit spirit of adoption. Christians can't help it. It is hard-wired into Christian nature and mandated in Christian nurture. Welcomed by God as strangers and adopted as children, churches and congregations have been communities for embodying this practice ever since. The adopted become adopters. Because, in God's eyes, we are all adoptees – the people God chose to take to heart, and to make a home with, and to spend eternity in the many-roomed mansion of God.

This is one of those deep, inchoate, value-laden dynamics that meant the Church could never be a sect or a cult from the outset. It was always bound to be, deeply, a foundation for society: the open, adopting *oikos* is a vision of how to live together, not just how to be church.

That is why the churches, at their best, function like adoption and foster homes: they welcome the unwelcome; they love the unloved; they embrace the excluded. The church was not meant to be a cult or a club for members, any more than the Christian vision for 'family' was ever meant to be 'nuclear'. It wasn't.

The early church took in widows and orphans. The early church was extensive and open in character. It embraced slave and free, Jew and Gentile. It will have embraced married and unmarried, and young and old, citizen and alien. If the Church wants to recover a vision for mission and evangelism, and plead for the restoration of moral foundations in contemporary society, then appealing to the sanctity of the 'nuclear family' is not the way forward.

Instead, the way forward is to recognize that by receiving, welcoming and incorporating the alien and the stranger into our households, it is as though we are receiving Christ. The act of reception and incorporation blesses the receiving-host as much as the recipient-guest. The lesson for the churches today could hardly be clearer: 'It is in giving that we receive.'

Yes, this is *pseudepigrapha*, I know. For the phrase is not to be found in the Scriptures at all, but was rather uttered by St Francis of Assisi over a millennium later. This was Francis' own interpretation of Jesus' proclamation for the radically inclusive-incorporative kingdom of God. It is by opening our hearts and doors to others that we not only bless them but are in turn blessed *by* them. And then we are blessed again by God for acting in the way that Jesus both teaches and embodies: loving, welcoming and inclusive to all.

Can a Eunuch be Baptized?
Reading Acts 8

EMMA PERCY

The church I attended from the age of eight until I went to train for ordination in my early twenties was a very ordinary Anglican parish church. I say that, but as I look back I realize that it was an unusually inclusive community. We were a diverse bunch. My own family was single-parent headed by my father.

Amid the mix of unusual family patterns and interesting characters was one person who I would now identify as intersex. Intersex is a loose term that covers those born with 'ambiguous' genitalia, those who have chromosomal conditions that do not conform to the common XX or XY configuration or other endocrine conditions which affect development of reproductive organs. Sometimes he dressed as Ted, the name he had been given as a child and had used for most of his life. Other times she was Hazel.

He explained one day, to my slightly embarrassed teenage self, that he had been born with a micro penis: enough to identify him as a boy. Yet at puberty nothing really happened. He moved into adulthood with an unbroken voice and little change in his genitals. At last, in his sixties there was a feeling that this non-conforming body could live out a non-conforming lifestyle expressing through name and dress the mix of identities that Ted/Hazel felt. At church we just took our clue from the clothing and used the name that went with the clothes.

It seems that the Church of England has been debating the

question of gender for a long time. However, the debates, which have been so fixated on what roles women can occupy, have only just begun to address the realities of people like Ted/ Hazel. The Church has assumed that the main issue is whether women can do things that men have traditionally done, and the deeper complexity of how we understand gender has largely gone unexamined. The subject of sex and gender is much more complex. There is now a wider recognition that some people defy neat biological definitions of sex. There is also an increasing awareness of those who feel that the bodily sex they inhabit is not the gender that they are.

Intersex bodies challenge accepted views of biological determinism. Questions of transgender unsettle not just traditional ideas about gender binaries but also feminist ideas about the social construction of gender. Some prominent feminists, including Germaine Greer, have been vilified for questioning whether a trans woman is a woman. Recent headlines have questioned at what point someone is a woman: when she chooses to live identifying as one or when her body has been physically altered? Should a pre-op trans woman be placed in a male or female prison? Though these binary-confusing realities affect a minority of individuals, they pose questions for us all about the continued limitations of neat gender definitions.

The difficulty is that we are still wedded to the language of gender binaries, of male or female. Feminism has challenged assumptions that define women as essentially opposite or complementary to men, affirming women's abilities to enter what were previously considered male spaces of education, work and lifestyle. Yet, feminists in campaigning for women's equality have needed to practise what Serene Jones calls 'strategic essentialism', arguing that women's difference needs to be represented in these places and that the invisibility of women in so many important spheres is detrimental to their experiences and opportunities.[1] Feminism has sought to dismantle gender binaries, but, in campaigning for women's rights, it has also needed to use them.

This is true in the theological debates as well. There is a

tension between the rightful emphases of our common human identity, made in the image of God, and the need to find specifically feminine language and imagery to affirm women as visibly present in our understanding of God and salvation. It is all too easy to fall into the language of soft complementarianism and to continue to perpetuate binary ideas about the God-givenness of being male or female.

We change brethren to brothers and sisters, affirm that men and women are made in the image of God and allow women, with appropriate caveats, to hold office and speak the words of God liturgically. We read Galatians 3.28, 'in Christ there is no male and female', to mean that in Christ both men and women are acceptable rather than a potential pointer to the meaninglessness of such categories in the light of our new creation in Christ.

While it is inappropriate to try and read into biblical texts the kind of concerns we have about gender inclusion in the twenty-first century, it is fascinating to note that they are needed to engage with a different 'gender' issue. In Acts 8.26–40, early in the unfolding story of the Christian Church, we find an encounter between Philip the evangelist and a eunuch from Ethiopia. The inclusion of this story points to an interest in the question posed towards its end, 'What is to stop me being baptized?' or, as I have titled this piece, can a eunuch be baptized; can a eunuch become a new creation in Christ, part of the body of Christ?

Eunuchs were a reality in the first century. They were usually boys who had been 'castrated' at some level, pre-puberty, giving them an adult body which was neither fully male nor female but recognizably other. Jesus' words in Matthew 19 point to an awareness that some eunuchs were born with a condition that made them 'eunuch'-like, but the majority would have been deliberately castrated. As with this individual, they were most often servants or slaves within a royal household, though not simply there to guard harems; their level of responsibility was much wider. They often held high office, trusted because they could not have families of their own and thus were presumed to be loyal to their master or mistress. Within the Roman Empire a slave eunuch was a status symbol, a luxury high-end commodity. In the early church, with its inclusion of slaves, it is likely that some would have been eunuchs.

Here we have a eunuch who holds high office in the court of the Candace, the female ruler, of Ethiopia. Clearly the eunuch is an educated individual and deeply interested in the Jewish religion. Many commentators over the years have suggested that the term eunuch can simply be understood as referring to his job. Yet, Brittany Wilson notes that the term eunuch is used repeatedly throughout the story and other terms are used alongside it to describe his role: 'Luke's repeated designation of the character as "the eunuch" suggests that this designation is central and should thus be the guiding principle in our interpretation.'[2]

The encounter between Philip and the eunuch is edgy. It happens on a wilderness road and the eunuch is an Ethiopian serving a female ruler. Wilson notes that in Greco-Roman litera-ture Ethiopians were seen as distant people, either idealized or demonized. They were often associated with 'womanish' traits. The Ethiopian eunuch is someone who is an outsider, an other.

In terms of their setting, the eunuch and Philip are spatially 'betwixt and between': they are neither here nor there, but on a deserted road in the middle of the wilderness. As the ultimate boundary-crosser, the eunuch is from a nation that lies on the borders of the so-called civilized world and greets Philip on the borders of civilization itself. Wilson concludes:

Because of his primary identification as 'the eunuch', the eunuch emerges above all as a gender-liminal character ... the eunuch is neither male nor female, neither Jew nor Gentile, neither elite nor non-elite ... Luke lifts up a eunuch official, or impotent 'power', and points to Jesus' own impotent power as the suffering servant of Isaiah 53, the slaughtered and shorn lamb who is humiliated and exalted, crucified and risen.[3]

Philip finds the eunuch reading the passage from Isaiah 53 and at the end of their conversation, when Philip has shared the good news of Jesus as the fulfilment of Isaiah, the question is asked, 'What is to prevent me from being baptized?' Those listening might well respond that the problem is that we are talking about a eunuch. The Torah prohibits those who have been castrated or who do not have recognizable masculine genitalia from participating in worship: 'No one whose testicles are crushed or whose penis is cut off shall be admitted to the assembly of the LORD' (Deuteronomy 23.1). Leviticus 21.20 includes crushed testicles in a list of 'blemishes' that would prevent a descendant of Aaron from participating in their priestly role. It seems that crushing the testicles was a recognized method of castrating boys.

Yet, alongside these texts of exclusion there are more hopeful texts. Isaiah 56.1–5 speaks of salvation for both the foreigner and specifically the eunuch. The faithful eunuch will receive a place in God's house and 'a monument and a name better than sons and daughters' (Isaiah 56.5). The 'dry branch' – that the eunuch may see himself as – will, like so much that is dry and barren in Isaiah's imagery, become fruitful. In Wisdom 3.13–14 we find the faithful eunuch again promised blessing and fulfilment. Even Jesus seems to have spoken affirmatively about eunuchs, acknowledging their existence in Matthew 19.12.

So, can a eunuch be baptized? This passage in Acts is emphatic. No words are offered in response to the eunuch's question, just inclusive action. Philip baptizes the eunuch who then continues on his journey rejoicing. It seems that the Church welcomes in the outsider, and in baptism the eunuch finds a place in God's house accepted as he is and welcomed into the body of Christ. We can, I think, assume that the inclusion of this encounter in the book of Acts was a deliberate pointer to the inclusion of eunuchs into the baptized family of the Church. Those who were neither male nor female can find an equal identity within the new creative community of Christ.

How does reflecting on this encounter in Acts help us in

thinking about gender in today's Church? It is not appropriate simply to map the term 'eunuch' on to those who are intersex or transgender. We are living in a different time and with different gender questions. Yet, it is important for us to recognize and speak about the Bible stories of people who did not fit into the neat binaries of male and female. This can be a helpful scriptural challenge to our fixed ideas about gender. Recognizing that Daniel and his companions – Old Testament heroes of the lions' den and the fiery furnace – were probably eunuchs and provide positive examples of such liminal figures. They are described as young, good-looking boys from good households taken captive and trained for office in the Babylonian court by the head eunuch. The practice of taking young foreigners of good birth as spoils of war and making them eunuchs is well attested.

We should also note that Nehemiah, cupbearer to King Artaxerxes, was almost certainly a eunuch. He would be unlikely to hold the position if he was not. These are individuals used by God, blessed by God and held up as examples of faithfulness who did not conform to normative ideas of maleness, who existed in a liminal gender identity. And the prophecies in Isaiah and Wisdom point to this ideal of the faithful eunuch whom God will bless. These stories and prophecies need to be part of ordinary preaching, affirming that God works through those who might be considered different. I cannot count the number of sermons I have heard about the Ethiopian eunuch which have made no reference to the significance of his being a eunuch!

The Acts 8 story itself offers an important reminder to make inclusion a priority. Baptism becomes for the Church the mark of a Christian and, unlike circumcision, it does not require a particular gendered body. Women can be baptized and so too can those whose bodies do not conform to gender norms. This is all part of the good news of the community of Jesus Christ. What was true then is true now, and this has pastoral implications in caring for those who do not fit into our binary gender categories. We need to hold on to the priority of inclusion in the baptized family of the Church. Susannah Cornwall quotes Sally Gross, an intersex ex-priest,

> who was told by fellow Christians that her baptism was invalid since 'as she did not fall into either of the categories 'determinately male' or 'determinately female', she also did not fall into the category 'human' and was therefore not 'the kind of thing which could have been baptized validly'.[4]

This shows how easily an anthropology that is totally grounded in essentialist distinctions between men and women can become exclusive. Worse, it can, as this quote bears out, fail to acknowledge the full humanity of those who do not fit. Baptism does not need a specific kind of human body.

Clergy need to be aware of the pastoral needs of families with intersex babies who may want baptism before they feel they can assign a gender to their child. Registers ask for the child's sex, but surely this is not a necessary requirement of baptism. In a culture where children are often identified as male or female by scans, even before they are born, the families of those who cannot be so neatly categorized need compassionate pastoral support. Parents, wider families and friends may need creative language to help affirm the child. This includes positive assurances of God's love and blessing.

A number of intersex conditions only become apparent during puberty. Again, young people and families need those who can speak with affirmation about the rich diversity of humanity and, where necessary, affirm the inclusive nature of God's love. There may well be a sense of loss for those who discover at this stage that they are females without a womb or boys who will not experience a full transition into an adult male body. Our theological definitions of male and female are so deeply grounded in procreation, and those whose bodies are not made to easily reproduce challenge us to find positive religious language about who they are and how they are fruitful. They challenge us to think about what makes someone male or female.

Where intersex individuals challenge long-held assumptions about the 'natural' division of humanity into male or female, transgender individuals challenge understandings about the body and gender identity. For those, like me, who have been deeply shaped by feminism, gender reassignment appears to point to a failure of the challenge to gender norms; we see people associating particular bodies with particular gender identities. They appear to reinforce the sharp distinction between male and female while presenting a new way of inhabiting the gender with which they identify. We need to listen to those who have and are making such transitions and learn from them to reflect again on the complexity of human identity, and heed the work of groups such as Trans Anglicans, who reflect on faith and transgender issues. There are churches which welcome those who do not fit the gendered binaries, but many struggle to make an affirming space for those in transition. There needs to be greater theological education around these issues, and this will include the acknowledgement that we do not necessarily understand.

In practical terms, there are pastoral issues for those who change their baptismal names when they change their gender. We may well need to develop rituals around such changes. There are ongoing questions about marriage of those who now inhabit a gender different from that of their birth certificate. This is particularly difficult within the Church where current prohibitions of same-sex marriage are grounded in complementary views of men and women that see gender binaries as God given. In fact, the debates around sexuality often show unthinking assumptions about gender. Cornwall points out that in these debates intersex tends to be acknowledged as a rare disability to be treated with sympathy, while transgender identities are seen as a product of disordered thinking.[5]

It is important that writers, like Cornwall, have challenged the Church to recognize those who do not fit into our neat categories of male and female. The Church needs to learn from Philip in Acts and welcome in those of liminal gender. What these challenges also highlight is the continuing need for the Church to theologically examine its gender assumptions. Unfortunately, debates around what women can and cannot do in the Church, alongside debates about what gay and lesbian people are permitted to do, have led to adversarial rather than exploratory discussions of gender.

Much of the progress within the Church to allow women to hold office as priests and bishops has happened without a proper rethinking of these assumptions. While restrictively deterministic ideas of complementarity are held by a minority, many, including those who have argued for women's inclusion, still work from a soft complementary position grounded in a reading of Genesis 1.27 that maintains that men and women are different even if equal: to be a human person is to exist bodily as either a male or female and to relate to God and other people as such.

Alongside this, Galatians 3.28 has been read as allowing women to join men in the Church and not as a radical challenge to the way we understand being human. 'In Christ there is neither male nor female' can and should point us to the reality that in Christ these very human categories are undermined.

Yes, each of us is an embodied person who needs to live out our life within the particularity of our bodies. For many of us that may well mean we live in relationships that conform to normative social understandings of men and women. However, we need to do so in the knowledge that neatly defined gender identities do not work for everybody. We also need to resist the sense that Genesis 1 and 2 assume difference beyond procreation. As human beings we are made in the image of God (Genesis 1) and made for relationship with God and each other. As the Genesis 2 story tells us, Adam was delighted by the likeness of Eve. Here at last is someone who is bone of my bone, flesh of my flesh. And as we rejoice in the first creation, we rejoice too in the inclusive nature of the re-creation offered to all human beings in the person of Christ. There is no longer Jew or Greek, there is no longer slave or free, there is no longer male and female: for all of you are one in Christ.

Cornwall points out that our imagery of Christ and of God needs to reflect the diversity of humanity:

To assert that Christ is female, intersexed, disabled or of a variant ethnicity is to make a claim not about the historical human body of Christ (for he, like every other human, was limited to being some things to the exclusion of others), but about what Christ (and God in Christ) has become since, in and through the human members of the Body ... It is just as Christ like to be intersexed and impaired as it is to be male and able-bodied.[6]

In our understanding of humanity, we need to move beyond neat categorizations and in our depictions of the body of Christ we need to include all those from that Ethiopian eunuch onwards who have been baptized into its reality.

Notes

1 Serene Jones, *Feminist Theory and Christian Theology: Cartographies of Grace*, Minneapolis, MN: Fortress Press, 2000.

2 Brittany Wilson, 'Neither Male nor Female', *New Testament Studies* 60 (2014), pp. 403–22, p. 418.

3 Wilson, 'Neither Male nor Female', p. 422.

4 Susannah Cornwall, '"What Religion or Reason Could Drive a Man to Forsake his Lover?" Relational Theology, Co-creativity and the Intersexed Body of Christ', in *Through Us, With Us, In Us*, ed. L. Isherwood and E. Bell Chambers, London: SCM Press, 2010, pp. 33–51, p. 41.

5 Susannah Cornwall, '"State of Mind" versus "Concrete Set of Facts": The Contrasting of Transgender and Intersex in Church Documents on Sexuality', *Theology and Sexuality* 15, no. 1 (September 2009), pp. 7–28.

6 Cornwall, '"What Religion or Reason"', p. 50.

Night Prayer

JIM COTTER

Mothering God, as I curl up in bed this night, I call upon
your blessed Spirit to be with me. The pains of the day are
many, and the aches in my heart overwhelm. You draw me
to you, you have taught me to pray, yet all I have are tears
and sadness.

Mothering God, as you held the pain of Jesus in Gethsemane,
hold my pain now. Give me relief where there is no earthly
relief to be found. Give me peace where only the peace of
your Spirit may prevail. Give me wisdom to know what
should travel onwards with me, and what to leave here at the
threshold of the night.

Mothering God, she who birthed all, nurtures all, loves all.
Sing me to sleep tonight. Let me give my burdens to you as
you make your melodies over me. Carry my discomfort so I
may rest. If wakefulness lies ahead, wake with me. Be with
me. Assure me of your presence and imbue me with your
indulgent love.

Until the morning, until we rise, with the Spirit in our hearts
and glory in our eyes.

UNITED IN LOVE

Love, marriage, commitment and fidelity are cornerstones for the foundation of society. It is often assumed that Christian marriage is a given, and to the exclusion of all other kinds of union. The Bible says otherwise and is constantly introducing patterns of family life and partnership that model love, fidelity and longevity. In this section we explore and celebrate the different configurations of loving and sexual relations that also demonstrate the grace, kindness and fidelity of God in loving union. In an age when many ache for stable, faithful and loving partnerships – or to be raised within such families and homes – we offer these resources as a means of blessing, affirmation and hope.

Does the Bible Really Give Us a Clear Definition of Marriage?

MARTYN PERCY

'We all know that love is the answer', opined Woody Allen, 'but while you're waiting for the answer, sex raises some pretty good questions'.[1] Questions, indeed. And before we even begin to answer that question – 'Does the Bible really give us a clear definition of marriage?' – we might want to ask this: 'What kind of book is the Bible, and how should we read it?' The answer to that question will help us navigate the issue of 'biblical marriage'. So, let us begin at the beginning, and with some words from Dan Brown's bestselling novel *The Da Vinci Code*:

> Teabing smiled. 'Everything you need to know about the Bible can be summed up by the great Canon Dr Martyn Percy.' Teabing cleared his throat and declared, 'The Bible did not arrive by fax from heaven ... the Bible is a product of man, my dear. Not of God. The Bible did not fall magically from the clouds. Man created it as a historical record of tumultuous times, and it has evolved through countless translations and revisions. History has never had a definitive version of the book ... More than eighty gospels were considered for the New Testament, and yet only [four] were chosen for inclusion ... The Bible, as we know it today, was collated by the pagan Roman emperor Constantine the Great ...'[2]

Like so much else in Dan Brown's novel, this is not quite right. But speaking as the person quoted above, I'll try and clarify my views a little. It is true that 'the Bible is not a fax from heaven' is a quote correctly attributed to me, although to the best of my knowledge I have only ever said this in lectures, radio, TV and newspaper interviews – and always in connection with how to understand fundamentalism. Furthermore, behind the slick sound bite, there is a fairly sophisticated theological point. So let me explain.

Views about the authority of Scripture cannot be directly resourced from the Bible itself. The Bible has no self-conscious identity. As a collation of books and writings, it came together over a long period of time. Indeed, the word 'bible' comes from the Greek *biblos*, simply meaning 'books'. Equally, the word 'canon' (here used in relation to Scripture, not as an ecclesiastical title) simply means 'rule'.

So the Scriptures are, literally, 'authorized books'. The authorization of the compilation took place some time after the books were written. When Paul wrote 'All scripture is *inspired* by God' (2 Timothy 3.16) in a letter to his friend, Timothy, he could hardly have had his own letter in mind at the time. The conferral of canonical status on his letter came quite a bit later – and some would say much later.

Views on the authority of the Bible cannot be solely resourced from itself. The Bible needs to be held and understood in a particular way, independent of its content, in order to have any authority. For some (I'm thinking here of fundamentalists), the power of God must be mediated through clear and pure identifiable channels or agents. This guarantees the quality of that power: it is unquestionable and unambiguous.

But for others – usually of a more mainstream, broad persuasion – God acts and speaks through channels and agents that are fully themselves. So God works through culture, peoples and history, not over and against them. The almighty power of God is only ever known on earth partially (not absolutely); it can only be encountered 'through a glass darkly' and not 'face to face'. Yet.

Although the power of God may be pure and absolute at source, God *always* chooses to mediate that power through less than perfect agents (such as language, people, times and places). This is because God's primary interest is in disclosing love in order to draw us into relationships, and not in unequivocal demonstrations of power that would leave no room for a genuinely free response, merely obedience in the face of oppression. So we have the burning bush for Moses – but he covers his face. And although Jesus is the light of the world, 'the darkness comprehends it not', according to John. What is revealed is still 'hidden' to those who are blind.

So, some Christians believe that Scripture has come from heaven to earth, in an unimpaired, totally unambiguous form – like a 'fax'. Such views are fundamentalist: the Bible is the pure word of God – every letter and syllable is 'God-breathed'. There is no room for questions; knowledge replaces faith. It is utterly authoritative: to question the Bible is tantamount to questioning God. The Bible here is more like an instruction manual than a mystery to be unpacked. It teaches plainly and woe to those who dissent.

But to those who believe that Scripture is a more complex body of writings, the authority of Scripture lies in the total witness of its inspiration. Thus, the Bible does indeed contain many things that God may want to say to humanity (and they are to be heeded and followed). But it also contains opinions about God (even one or two moans and complaints – see the psalms); it contains allegory, parables, humour, histories and debates. The nature of the Bible invites us to contemplate the very many ways in which God speaks to us. The Bible is not one message spoken by one voice. It is, rather, *symphonic* in character, a restless and inspiring chorus of testaments, whose authority rests upon its very plurality. The Scriptures are like sausages – delicious, nourishing and tasty – but you really don't want to see how they are made.

Yes, the Bible is revered holy Scripture. But blind obedience to all of Scripture is not practised by any group of Christians known to me, or who have ever lived. Few Christians abstain from eating black pudding on scriptural grounds (Acts 15.28–29). Few Christians follow the Levitical texts on dress codes to the letter, if at all. I do know of Christians who object to clapping in worship (it is of the 'old covenant'; that is, not mentioned in the New Testament). I know of other Christians who object to most kinds of dancing on the same ticket. Then there is slavery. While not exactly praised to the hilt in Scripture, it is condoned and never censured – a fact not lost on the Confederate Christians who fought in the American Civil War.

Indeed, the recent HBO television adaptation of Margaret Atwood's *The Handmaid's Tale* (1985) gives us a rich and interesting insight into what 'biblical marriages' can look like. In Atwood's fictional Republic of Gilead, set in some future dystopia, the adult female population is divided between handmaids, Marthas and wives. The function of the handmaids was to bear children to the master of the house. Marthas are there to serve. Wives are to submit. This is a 'biblical marriage' pattern, of sorts.

Abraham thought he and Sarah could not have children, and so they turned to Hagar, their Egyptian handmaid (Genesis 16). Is this a biblical pattern of marriage? It is to such questions that the author Rachel Held Evans turned her mind some years ago in her bestselling and also rather controversial book, *A Year of Biblical Womanhood* (2012).

Evans, intrigued by the traditionalist resurgence that had led many of her friends to abandon their careers to assume traditional gender roles in the home, decided to try it for herself. Adopting all of the Bible's instructions for women as literally as possible, she embarked on a radical life experiment, namely living a year of biblical womanhood. She grew her hair, adopted a 'gentle and quiet spirit' (1 Peter 3.4), covered her head, abstained from gossip, rose every day before dawn, made sure she 'praised her husband at the city gates' by holding up a cardboard sign saying 'Dan is awesome' on the main road leading into town(!), remained silent in church (of course) and also slept outside the family home during menstruation.

I have a hunch that the phrase 'biblical marriage' is similar to 'nuclear family'. It sounds biblical enough. Yet neither of these phrases is found in the Bible. Perhaps that is why in 2014 my wife (Emma) and I responded with such alacrity to an invitation to write an introduction for the NRSV wedding gift Bible. It was a joy to write together, but in sending off the final text, I included a note to the publisher. I said that, in the spirit of the NRSV translation, we had avoided using gendered pronouns for God where possible. And we had also done the same for the individuals who were getting married. So you could give this Bible to any couple. Yes, any. So two women, or two men, could receive the gift of holy Scripture to celebrate their marriage. The Bible is for everyone, after all.

The Bible, as the word of God, and as a single book, is a collection of Scriptures that speak to us in many different ways about God, love and life. It is not one voice, but many; yet though many, one. And that one message is this: that God is love and those who live in love live in God and God lives in them (1 John 4.16). So the Bible itself is a covenant sign. It is a marriage – a union of Scriptures – that can only be understood in the totality of its witness. And that is partly why I am so committed to same-sex marriages. I see no reason why such unions cannot reflect the love of God and bear testimony to God's grace, truth and power.

I am always wary of groups or individuals who claim to be 'biblical', because in my experience this kind of exclusive, tribal claim is exactly the kind of thing the Bible doesn't offer us. In fundamentalist worlds, it is never the Bible that rules; it is always the interpreter. That's why we read Scriptures together – because this is a shared journey of adventure and discovery in which the simple can confound the wise, and the foolish outwit the clever.

I know it is not easy for some Christians to see God at work in a same-sex marriage, and some may never be able to. But these days a growing number can and do; they see all marriages as something to celebrate. They see that Scripture does not lay down one pattern of marriage, like an instruction manual. Rather, marriage, like Scripture, is a mystery to be unpacked over time. In ongoing contemplation and appreciation, it can be a real sign of God's love and grace.

So Scripture – like art, music, poetry, symbols and signs – invites us to sit awhile and contemplate how God is revealed. The burning bush of Moses has no single meaning, and never could. The Bible offers several patterns of marriage. A loving marriage is a sacramental token of love and an invitation to pause and attend, stepping through the gate of mystery that God gives to us.

On the question of same-sex marriage, we may need reminding of one thing. God did not send us a fax. Instead, God chose to speak through Jesus – the body language of God – to remind us that God is ultimate love, and that those who live in love live in God and God lives in them. Sex raises some interesting questions, for sure. But so far as God is concerned, love is always the answer.

Notes

1 Woody Allen, Interview, *New York Times*, 1 December 1975.
2 Dan Brown, *The Da Vinci Code*, London: Bantam Press, 2003, chapter 55.

Celebrating Christian Marriage

Emma and Martyn Percy wrote this prologue together for the NRSV wedding gift Bible.[1] Where possible, they used inclusive pronouns so that the Scriptures could be given to any couple as a wedding gift. This is an extract.

Each marriage is unique; each partnership distinctive; no two unions are the same. Two individuals make solemn vows of commitment to each other – in words that have become so very familiar to us, yet remain unfailingly moving. The marriage vows promise 'love and cherishing' for an uncertain future. There will be times of 'for better and for worse', 'richer and poorer', and 'in sickness and in health'. It is the beginning of a journey in which each commits to being the faithful travelling companion of the other. There will be pleasant places and rocky terrain; gentle rises and steep slopes; and at different stages each may need to help the other. The goal of marriage is not merely to live life 'happily ever after'. But that rather, together, we will commit to enjoying each other in facing the ups and downs that life brings – in faithfulness and love.

Journeying is a central theme of the Bible. From Abraham in Genesis through to Paul in the New Testament, we read of men and women who have journeyed – trusting that God is their unfailing travelling companion. We read of better times in which blessings abound, and in which individuals and communities know what it means to be loved and cherished by God. The Bible is also clear about the difficult times when internal and external factors lead to wilderness experiences, and to some turbulent times in relationships. In these we learn more about human failings, God's forgiveness, and the way that detours from the path can become routes back into grace.

This is one of the many reasons why a Bible might be an appropriate gift for a couple about to commit their lives to each other. The Bible, as the word of God, and as a single book, is a collection of Scriptures that speak to us in many different ways about God, love and life. It is not one voice, but many and, though many, one message – that God is love, and those who live in love live in God, and God abides in them (1 John 4.16).

The psalms testify to the seasons of the heart in relation to God and the world. Many of the great, epic stories of individuals introduce us not only to people of remarkable faith and courage, but also to those same people who are fallible and need forgiveness. The Scriptures take us through winters and summers in our relationship with God, and spring and autumn in our spirituality. The Bible teaches us explicitly about relationships. But it also coaxes us implicitly.

Indeed, the Bible itself is a marriage. It is a marriage – a union of Scriptures – that can only be understood in totality. In its blend, it blesses. It contains love and hate; jealousy and fidelity. But it is not a book of mixed messages. Rather, it has one message to say through many voices. The authority of Scripture lies in the totality of its testament. The Bible contains opinions about God (even one or two moans and complaints – you only have to read the psalms!); it contains allegory, parables, humour, histories and debates.

In other words, the very nature of the Bible invites us to contemplate the many ways in which God speaks to us, which are open to a variety of interpretations. It is a book that unfolds, a journey that explores in numerous ways the loving commitment of God and the human attempts to respond to that love. The Bible is symphonic in character – a restless and inspiring chorus of testaments – the authority of which rests in its rich diversity. Thus, the Bible does indeed contain many things that God may want to say to humanity (and they are to be heeded and followed).

A good marriage might be said to be symphonic; the many notes and rhythms of a relationship combining to create a single piece of music. The parts coming together to make the whole; two become one. And this is what this marriage Bible celebrates – the many seasons, moods and notes of a marriage, bound as one.

Wedding vows are made face to face. The couple look at each other, hands clasped, as they speak the words of commitment. In marriage, a couple are promising to look at each other for the rest of their lives, and to be looked at: lovingly, faithfully and, above all, truly and honestly. Marriage is about the freedom to know another and be known: '*All that I am I give to you and all that I have I share with you.*'

Yet we know our human frailties and at times our inabilities to be honest with each other or even ourselves. In the wonderful description of love in First Corinthians 13, so often read in wedding services, we are reminded that the journey of faith leads to the place where we shall see God face to face and know as we are known. Clear and unobstructed: God's gaze upon us, full of love.

Understanding the love and knowledge that God has for us can help us to be more realistic and generous as we give ourselves to each other. Paul says that this loving commitment is a sign of Jesus' love for the Church, the body of Christ. The embodied love of marriage involves trusting our physicality to the other so that at some level our body becomes the other's, not in an objectifying act of possession but in the open and trusting generosity of love. The Bible writers use the verb 'to know' to convey both the physical and emotional aspects of marriage. We are known as an entirety of body and mind. To be known as we are is to be loved, and to be loved is to be truly known.

The word sometimes used for 'know' in the psalms – *yada* – (see Psalm 139) is a Hebrew word that means both knowledge and love. There can be no real love without truth. Equally, there can be no truth without love. Without trust and tenderness, truth can hide behind walls of fear and wells of pain.

Marriage presents to us, more clearly than any other kind of relationship, that there must be a unity between truth and love, between charity and clarity. Marriage calls us to a union that speaks of God's intended unity between humanity and divinity.

Yet love is not static. It must grow and change, just as our perceptions of truth will alter and deepen. Unveiling our faces, our minds, spirits and our bodies to each other and to God is a way of growth. In moments of strain or delight, hollowness or generosity, we are promised that 'for richer or for poorer' we shall be made more like Christ. Marriage is not a panacea: it does not make everything right, and fix what might be broken. In marriage, we take all of ourselves into a new relationship. Marriage is a particular kind of commitment to work out the differences, and to see them through. But it requires patience and forbearance. A wedding only commences a marriage: you have the rest of your lives to make it work.

And then there is a time and season for everything (see Ecclesiastes 3.1–8). Marriages develop habits and rhythms; celebration and consolation; truth and trust. Because love is patience and kindness, it accepts us as we are while knowing that love and truth transform us. It is something that grows and, in due season, its own fruits spread out and can be shared with others. Marriage is a gift of God in creation. So it takes ordinary people and, from them, can make extraordinary unions.

The idea that God uses fairly unpromising or unusual material for further purposes should not surprise us. In the Gospels, even miracles begin with ordinary, simple things. A child's packed lunch (Matthew 14.13–21) – a very ordinary thing – needs to be prepared, packed, lugged up a hillock and then offered before anything can happen to help feed 5,000 people. To catch some fish (John 21), someone needs to build a boat and make some nets.

In the miracle of the wedding at Cana in Galilee (John 2—11), we are given a story rich in analogy and symbolism. Most people remember the story of the wedding of Cana in Galilee for the end result – an absurd amount of very good wine produced at the end of a feast. Yet consider this: for the miracle of the wedding of Cana in Galilee to happen at all, two people had to take the risk of falling in love, and declare that they wanted to spend the rest of their natural lives together. To make water into wine, several people had to draw and fetch large amounts of water. To make the huge jars which contained the water, and later the miraculous wine, someone had to dig the clay, stoke the oven, mould the clay and fire it. And someone had the final headache of organizing a Jewish wedding reception for hundreds of guests.

Without these basic ordinary materials and effort, there would have been no miracle at Cana. We all have our part to play in the transformations and miracles that are wrought of God. And so it is with us. In marriage, God takes hold of us and begins something new. Relationships, when offered to God, become transformed in the union of marriage. In blessing – whether it is bread, wine, water or people – the ordinary is made extraordinary: a vehicle for grace. So it is in marriage, where through blessing, God fashions a relationship that is more than the sum of its parts. And yet it is import-ant to remember that we remain as we are, even as we are transformed.

Any marriage can be a testimony to what God does with simple, ordinary ingredients. At Cana-in-Galilee, common, local water is turned into wine. The transformation of what is basic is the key to the story of blessing. It draws out the very best of what that life or material is, to a new and redeemed status. Put another way, Jesus' attendance at the wedding in Cana is the blessing of reality. The ordinariness of marriage is something that God not only blesses but enters into the joy of at Cana. The marriage of two people is something that delights God.

Our Christian faith starts with realizing that God is already with us. And that just as God joins us in our lives, God invites us to join in that divine life that leaves nothing unseen, nothing unfelt, nothing unloved. God enters into our lives through the deepest covenant. God loves us more than we can ever know.

That commitment and love is total, and overwhelming. But it begins in the mundane, with Jesus with us in the normal everyday business of living, learning and loving. Christian faith is often the taking of ordinary people – with their own special and unique qualities – and it is allowing them to see that they can become instruments of God's blessing to us. It brings couples together in a blessed unity as the ordinary is made extraordinary.

God, through Jesus' hallowing of the wedding at Cana, is reminding us that it is here, in the ordinary, that we are met – in the plainest things: bread, wine ... and people. And, yes, even in wedding receptions. This is why the apostle Paul's well-known phrase is so important to remember: 'power is made perfect in weakness' (2 Corinthians 12.9). As the mystics say, if God has one weakness, it is God's heart: it is too soft. God loves to enter our lives on our level and, in so doing, draw us into that deeper experience of divine life that we can only know when we surrender to another – and to God.

That's why our Scriptures testify to one simple truth: it will all turn out fine if you are turned over to God. All you need do is reflect and embody some of the love that has already been shown to you. Love is the lesson. As William Langland put it in *The Vision of Piers Plowman* (c. 1370):

> 'Counseilleth me, Kynde', quod I, 'what craft be beste to lerne?'
> 'Lerne to love,' quod Kynde, 'and leef alle othere.'

God does not mind what kind of material there is to work with, as long as it is pliable. And a marriage is a call – a vocation, indeed – to become supple with each other. A marriage is a call to love another, as we grow and develop as individuals, and grow and develop in union. In marriage, we begin a work of building, redemption and completion. Two become one, and one is a new creation both on and through which God pours blessings. For it is in surrender to each other – the covenant that is made in a marriage – that we glimpse something of how

God works in the world. It is in giving and yielding that we also receive.

* * *

Some readings

God wills union because God did not make us to be alone. God made us for company and companionship; for the mutual learning that only a true, deep love can bring. God wills union, because God loves us first, before we can love God. As the Gospel says, unequivocally, 'Love one another as I have loved you' (John 15.12). Because God's love for us is complete, abundant and overwhelming. And it is from God's open heart and God's open hands that we are all embraced, and are invited to embrace one another. In marriage, we learn again that God loves us and has called us in our new union to share and proclaim that love.

It takes years to marry completely two hearts, even of the most loving and well assorted. A happy wedlock is a long falling in love. Young persons think love belongs only to the brown-haired and crimson-cheeked. So it does for its beginning but the golden marriage is a part of love which the bridal day knows nothing of ...[2]

The meaning of marriage begins in the giving of words. We cannot join ourselves to another without giving our word. And this must be an unconditional giving, for in joining ourselves to one another we join ourselves to the unknown. We must not be misled by the procedures of experimental thought: in life, in the world, we are never given two known results to choose between, but only one result: that we choose without knowing what it is...

Because the condition of marriage is worldly and its meaning communal, no one party to it can be solely in charge. What you alone think it ought to be, it is not going to be. Where you alone think you want it to go, it is not going to go. It is going where the two of you – and marriage, time, life, history and the world – will take it. You do not know the road: you have committed your life to a way.[3]

Many more are available at www.hitched.co.uk; for example, Louis de Bernières, *Captain Corelli's Mandolin* (London: Secker & Warburg Ltd, 1994).

Notes

1 Martin and Emma Percy, 'What Christian Marriage Means', *Holy Bible: NRSV Celebrating Christian* Marriage, London: SPCK, 2015, pp. III–VII.

2 Theodore Parker, 'The Divine Presence in Nature and in the Soul', *The Dial* 1, no. 1 (July 1840), pp. 58–70.

3 Wendell Berry, 'Poetry and Marriage: The Use of Old Forms', *Co-Evolution Quarterly* (Winter 1982), pp. 3–8.

A Celebration Service for N and N

JIM COTTER

This is a service of blessing and dedication for a couple who are making a lifelong commitment – either through a civil cere-mony, marriage or taking vows of union. It is purposefully set in the context of Holy Communion, so that the couple can gather together and share in the Eucharist with friends, family and witnesses. It reminds us that God is present in joy, sharing, celebration and self-gift – and that God delights in love. Always.

Entrance Music

N *and* N *enter together*

Welcome

We are here today to celebrate two people coming together to publicly declare their love and commitment to one another to those dearest to them. They understand that to be successful as a couple, requires the support and love of those around them – that's you!
This is the day that the Lord has made!
Let us rejoice and be glad in it.
It is good to give thanks to the Lord.
For his love endures for ever.

Hymn

Some suitable hymns:

- All my hope on God is founded
- Be thou my vision
- Come to a wedding, come to a blessing
- Jesu, thou joy of loving hearts
- Let us build a house where love can dwell (Marty Haugen)
- Lord and lover of creation
- Lord Jesus Christ, invited guest and Saviour
- Love divine, all loves excelling
- Love that wilt not let me go
- The grace of life is theirs
- We pledge to one another

Prayer

Loving and gracious God, who made us in your image and
sent your Son Jesus Christ to welcome us home; protect us in
love and empower us for service. May N and N continue to
be living signs of his love and may we uphold them in their
lives together. **Amen.**

Brothers and sisters, we meet here in the presence of God to
celebrate with N and N and to affirm their commitment to
each other. We join with them in their rejoicing and offer
them support with our love and prayers.
The step N and N have taken is much like a covenant,
which is an ancient form of promise, a public declaration of
commitment that binds people in an enduring relationship
through good and bad. The Bible tells the story of God's
incredible covenant with human beings, to choose them for
himself, to love them unconditionally and always to be there
for them.
All Christians are called to bear witness to the good news of
God's love and grace in Jesus Christ, through the power of

the Holy Spirit. We are empowered for such witness by our
covenantal relationship with God.
Baptism initiates us into that covenant, making us Christ's
own for ever and members of Christ's body, the Church. The
Eucharist sustains us in that covenantal life and strengthens
us to be Christ's witnesses in the world.
Our covenantal life with God is expressed in relationships of
commitment and faithfulness, to pray for God's grace in our
shared witness to the gospel in the world.

Reading or poem

(see www.hitched.co.uk for a wide range of choices)

Hymn

Affirmation

Please stand to affirm the covenant between *N* and *N*. Please
respond as you feel able with the words in **bold**.
For the darkness is as light. It's been a long road to travel to
bring about the recent changes in the law and attitudes that
now acknowledge the value and the rights and responsibilities
of relationships like *N* and *N*.
Many have suffered pain and anguish along the way to
achieve this. Enough people have loved and cared enough to
work towards the end of the oppression of gay people in this
country. Great strides have now been made towards that end.
Do you celebrate this?
We celebrate!
N and *N* have worked hard to make their relationship work;
they have been ready to adapt to change; they have welcomed
many into their lives and their home; they have sought to
contribute positively to their own communities. They stand

here now, rejoicing in the beauty, the fun and the love their partnership provides. Do you rejoice in this?
We rejoice!
They know that they have only managed this, and can only continue to achieve such a quality of life, through the love and support of their families and friends. They are deeply grateful for this, and wish only to see it continue, flourish and thrive. Will you support them, as they live together for as many years as they possibly can?
We will support them!

Promises

(N) Today is mostly an ordinary day: the sun rose, people travelled, food was prepared, people greeted one another, and we just so happen to be celebrating our love.
(*Where a civil marriage has already taken place*) On *date* we made promises to each other for the rest of our days; no matter how ordinary or unusual they may be.
(N and N) I promised:
(N) to always laugh with you and to never go to bed angry.
(N) to comfort you in times of sorrow.
(N) to always listen to what you have to say, even when we don't see eye to eye,
(N) and to remember that love is saying, 'I feel differently'; instead of, 'You are wrong';
(N and N) to continue to love your children as if they were my own; as I am officially your partner in their lives.
(N) But most of all, I promised to love you, under any circumstances; happy or sad, easy or difficult,
(N) through the sunshine and through the rain for the rest of my days.
(N) I am the luckiest *man/woman*
(N) and I can't imagine growing old with anyone else.

Prayer

Heavenly Father, we pray that these rings, already given to
each other, be to N and N symbols of unending love and
faithfulness and a reminder of the promises they made to each
other: through Jesus Christ our Lord.
Amen.

Prayers for N and N

Loving Father, we give thanks and praise to you for your
unfailing love and generosity to us: the gift of our lives and
the joy of human love.
We give you thanks and praise for N and N.
You have created in them the desire for intimacy,
companionship and faithfulness. You have called them out of
isolation.
You have strengthened them against prejudice and fear, and
surrounded them with family and friends who love them.
Pour out your love upon them as they grow in their love for
one another. May they find gladness in each other, in mutual
giving and receiving.
May they bring to each other generosity, compassion and
forgiveness as they share their joys and their sufferings, their
fears and their hopes.
Lead them into accomplishments that satisfy and delight.
Shower them with your gifts of wisdom, patience and
courage, that their love may be a source of happiness and
their home a place of welcome for all who are their guests.
And be with them, that in the years ahead they may be
faithful to the promises they have made this day; that they
may grow together in love, joy, peace and wisdom.
We ask all this in the name of Jesus Christ their Lord, who
with you and the Holy Spirit lives and reigns, one God, now
and for ever.
Amen.

Confession

God our Father,
we have sinned against you and against one another,
we have not loved you with all our heart
we have not loved our neighbour as ourselves.
But you have kept faith with us.
Have mercy on us, forgive us our sins
and restore us to newness of life,
through Jesus Christ our Lord.
Amen.

Absolution

May God who loved the world so much that he sent his Son
to be our Saviour, forgive us our sins and make us holy to
serve him in the world, through Jesus Christ our Lord.
Amen.

Readings

Old Testament reading: Song of Songs 8.6–7
Gospel: Luke 24.13–35

Sermon

Hymn

Eucharist

The Lord be with you.
And also with you.
Lift up your hearts.
We lift them to the Lord.
Let us give thanks to the Lord our God.
It is right to give him thanks and praise.

It is indeed right, our duty and our joy at all times and in
   all places.
But on this day we give you thanks
that you have brought us to life.
For you have made us in your own image,
shaping us with infinite care, as creatures of delight and passion,
setting us in a world of every good thing,
a world of our giftedness.

It is right and our joy to give you thanks,
for you sent Jesus to walk about among us sharing
   our humanity,
One whom even death could not stop,
knowing with us the bodily pain and hurt
as integrity is trampled in the dust
and justice dissolves in empty words.

It is right and our joy to give you thanks,
for you are present with us in the Spirit,
provoking us, lifting us, nudging us
to work for the healing of this world's brokenness,
to keep alive the dreams and visions of a world
where all are valued, where God may look
from heaven and see that all is good, that all is very good.
And so today in the company of each other
and in company with people throughout the world
we declare as generations before us have declared.

Holy, Holy, Holy, Lord, God of power and might.
Heaven and earth are full of your glory.
Hosanna in the highest.
Blessed is he who comes in the name of the Lord.
Hosanna in the highest.

God has brought us to this table.
We come, remembering that night among friends,
the night of terrible betrayal, when Jesus took bread,
blessed it, broke it and shared it saying:

Take eat, this is my body
which is given for you.
Do this to remember me.
And taking the cup of wine, he gave thanks and said:
Drink this all of you; this is the blood of my covenant
poured out for you.
Come, Holy Spirit, be present here in the mystery of
this Eucharist;
lead us out to follow the risk-taking Christ.

The Lord's Prayer

Our Father who art in heaven,
Hallowed be thy name.
Thy kingdom come,
thy will be done,
on earth as it is in heaven.
Give us this day our daily bread.
And forgive us our trespasses,
as we forgive those who trespass against us.
And lead us not into temptation,
but deliver us from evil.
For thine is the kingdom,
the power, and the glory,
for ever and ever. Amen.

We break this bread remembering the brokenness of our world
and declaring our hope of wholeness and declaring our
shalom is in Christ.
We poured this wine remembering the pain and bloodshed
of our world and declaring our hope in the overflowing love
of Christ.

As the table is prepared, this or another suitable song is sung:
Shalom my friends

Distribution

Suggested music during the distribution:

- I watch the sunrise
- Let love be real

Post-communion prayer

Eternal God, comfort of the afflicted and healer of the
broken, you have fed us at the table of life and hope: teach
us the ways of gentleness and peace, that all the world may
acknowledge the kingdom of your Son Jesus Christ our Lord.

Final hymn

Gathering around the church in a circle we say together:
A circle has no beginning and no end, which is why we
symbolically stand here in a circle, to show to *N* and *N* our
never-ending love and support. We pledge to continue to
uphold you in your journey together. We wish you much joy,
rich blessings and deep contentment in your lives together.
Now may the Lord bless you and keep you; the Lord make
his face to shine upon you and be gracious unto you, the Lord
turn his face toward you and give you peace.

Blessing of the couple

There is a place of peace,
a place of wisdom, a place of love.
May this sacred centre be your guide.
May it be to you strength for the journey.
May it fill you with hope when all seems hopeless.
And may it lead you to know the sacredness in all.

May life bring enough challenge to fuel your dreams, enough affirmation to honour your gifts, and nurture to give your spirit peace.

Believe in your vision. Follow your dreams.

May you be brave enough to expose to each other your aching woundedness and reveal your vulnerability.

May you speak your deepest truths, knowing that they will change as you do.

May you love even though your heart breaks again and again. And until the end of your days, may your life be filled with possibilities and courage.

May the spirit of constant change be ever renewing itself in your hearts,

pruning, composting and growing, that you may bear blossom and fruit.

And as you step forward into your next chapter, we send with you our fondest hopes and blessings.

Know always that, when you return to us, you will find the hands of friends.

Final blessing

As we have been blessed, so we bless one another to be a blessing. Breathe in, breathe out, this breath we share with all who breathe. Feel the love of God flowing through this community, into you, and out into the world. Let love – your love – flow outward, to its height, its depth, its broad extent. You are more than you know, and more loved than you know. Take up what power is yours to create safe haven, to make of earth a heaven. Give hope to those you encounter, that they may know safety from inner and outer harm, be happy and at peace, healthy and strong, caring and joyful. Be the blessing you already are.

May the love of God surround us,
may the peace of God assure us,
and may the blessing of God rest with us
until we meet again. Amen.

The Blessing of Civil Partnerships

*A celebration of commitment and blessing;
a covenant of profound friendship; a
ceremonial perspective*

JIM COTTER

A working text for a ceremony of commitment and blessing

Welcome

Welcome to this place, welcome to this time,
To be made sacred by our presence and our purpose.
Welcome to you, N and N, welcome to you, your families
and your friends.
Welcome in the name of the One who invites us all, not to be
slaves or servants but to be friends.

*The celebrant may well have first welcomed everybody more
informally than this, said something about the place where
you have gathered, and helped the company to be at ease. The
printed words may be a bridge between the informal welcome
and the more formal introduction that follows.*

A formal introduction to a ceremony of blessing

In the presence of the Living One, we have come together to give public witness and personal support to N and N, as they celebrate the love they have for each other, as they affirm and deepen their commitment to each other, and as they seek and receive blessings divine and human.

In this ceremony we remind ourselves of what it means to be human, which is to grow in love for the God of many names, for children, women and men with their many names, and for all the creatures to whom we have given so many names.

A ceremonial perspective: a ceremony of commitment and blessing

True love draws away from self as centre, and towards others in mutual giving and receiving, in respect and compassion. True love avoids all violation of others, whether by force or manipulation, by treating others as less than human or by exploiting the other's trust and goodwill.

From the earliest times men and women have made vows, promises that are solemn and sacred, affecting them for the rest of their lives ...

We recall the ancient stories of Ruth and Naomi, of David and Jonathan, of Sergius and Bacchus, of Aelred and Simon, and the contemporary stories of our own mothers and fathers, partners and friends.

We have travelled from near and far to witness this day another such exchange of vows.

More profoundly, our inner journeys to this time and place have often been by winding paths, difficulties and discoveries, with doubts and questions, with perplexity and patience, with trust and courage.

On those journeys we may also have come to believe that the Love, which is alive within us and among us, by whatever name, sees deep into the human heart, longs to bless N and

N, recognizes the love they have for each other, rejoices in the gift that each of them is making to the other, and yearns to see them flourish and grow in the warmth of that love, and to drench them with all that is good.

This formal introduction gently lowers one and all to a deeper level at which the key moments of the ceremony work them-selves into your being and touch memories in the hearts of those who watch and listen and bear witness.
A note to the celebrant: Don't rush. Give time for pauses. You may be familiar with this kind of occasion, but it is unique for the couple concerned. Also, make sure you emphasize the important words in each sentence, and avoid the common phenomenon, not least in religious circles, of emphasizing pronouns. This shows us that you are trying too hard, that you are imposing meaning on what you are saying, rather than giving sufficient colour to enable the meaning to be presented and received without strain.

Presentations

N, you have invited a member of your family and one of your friends to introduce you to this company and to present you this day to N.
N and N, I ask you now to do this ...
N, you have invited a member of your family and one of your friends to introduce you to this company and to present you this day to N.
N and N, I ask you now to do this ...

I first came across this custom at the celebration of a partner-ship between two men, one of whom was British, the other Filipino, among whose people such presentations are familiar. It helped families and friends to get to know at least a little about a person who was to most of them still a stranger.

Questions of intent

N and N, you are about to make a solemn promise. So that
each and all of us here may know of your intent, I ask you:
Do you believe that in God's love you have been drawn
together to live in ever-deepening love for each other?
We do.
Do you promise to be loyal to each other, never allowing any
other relationship to come before the one you are about to
affirm?
We do.
Will you give yourselves to each other wholeheartedly and
without reserve?
We will.
Will you recognize each other's freedom and allow each other
time and space to grow into that singular being each of us is
called to be?
We will.
Will you do all in your power to make your life together an
embodiment of the divine love in the world?
We will.
N, will you give yourself to N, sharing your love and your
life, your strengths and your weaknesses, your well-being and
your brokenness, your health and your sickness, your riches
and your poverty, your successes and your failures, through
all the days that are given to you?
I will.
N, will you give yourself to N, sharing your love and your
life, your strengths and your weaknesses, your well-being and
your brokenness, your health and your sickness, your riches
and your poverty, your successes and your failures, through
all the days that are given to you?
I will.

*You might like to think about the stance you take as you stand
next to each other and near the celebrant. Do you want to face
each other or face the celebrant? Or do you want to stand at*

an angle to each other, so that your head can move easily from the celebrant to your partner?

A note to the celebrant: Assuming that everybody present has a copy of the order of service in their hands, you can drop your voice, even switching off your microphone if you are using one, and speak quietly and directly to the couple. If you were really trained well, you can speak softly and also be heard at the back!

A covenant of profound and special friendship: the exchange of vows

In the wonderful mystery of God, Love-making Spirit between us, Pain-bearing Presence beside us, Life-giving Future before us, you, N, have been given to me, to be cherished in a profound and special friendship, to share with you all that I have and all that I am, with a loyalty to you that comes before all others.
Of my own free will I choose to share my life with you (and to care for such children as *are/may be* entrusted to us).
With and in that greater Love, and in the presence of these our witnesses,
I, N, affirm, renew, and deepen my promise to do all that I can for your well-being, N, to honour you as God's home, and to be loyal to you and full of faith in you, our life-day long.*

In the wonderful mystery of God, Love-making Spirit between us, Pain-bearing Presence beside us, Life-giving Future before us, you, N, have been given to me, to be cherished in a profound and special friendship, to share with you all that I have and all that I am, with a loyalty to you that comes before all others.
Of my own free will I choose to share my life with you (and to care for such children as *are/may be* entrusted to us).
With and in that greater Love, and in the presence of these our witnesses,

I, N, affirm, renew and deepen my promise to do all that I can for your well-being, N, to honour you as God's home, and to be loyal to you and full of faith in you, our life-day long.*

You may wish to replace the last line with, 'for as long as I shall live'. 'Our life-day long' is a poetic way of putting it, in fact it comes from W. H. Auden, and may of course be interpreted to mean 'for however long our love shall last'. This may be more honest, the first may be more daring. Ask, though, which kind of commitment most reflects that of God for us? (You may well comment, I'm not God, only doing all that I can to be the best human being I am capable of becoming.)

I think it works best for the vows and the rings that follow if the couple face each other rather than the celebrant. It also means that most people will be able to see at least their profiles!

The blessing of rings

God of generosity and bounty, bless these rings which we also bless in your name.
May N and N who will wear them recognize and cherish these symbols of the love that never ends.
May they find gladness in each other, in mutual giving and receiving, in the ringed dance of love.
May they be glad in the gift of themselves as bodies, in the touch that affirms and heals, that is affectionate and passionate, that unites and creates.
May they bring to each other tact and forbearance, compassion and forgiveness.
May they share their joys and their sorrows, their fears and their trust, and each give the other room to grow in freedom and in truth.

The exchange of rings

N, this ring is a symbol of never-ending love, of all that I am and all that I have.
Receive and treasure it as a token and pledge of the love I have for you.
Wear it always, and find in it a protection whenever we have to be apart.

N, this ring is a symbol of never-ending love, of all that I am and all that I have.
Receive and treasure it as a token and pledge of the love I have for you.
Wear it always, and find in it a protection whenever we have to be apart.

You might like to think of each ring being placed on a small cushion on a table, along with a candle by each. Between them you can put one larger candle. At the beginning of the ceremony, after the formal introduction, each of you could be given a lit taper from which to light each of the two outer candles. And after the exchange of rings, you could again take a taper, light it from your own candle, and together let the two tapers light the central candle. (Take care not to extinguish the outer candles, either your own or your partner's!) And let the candles have an honoured place in your home, lit each year on special anniversary days.

A prayer of offering

Living One, Creator and Lover of the world, we offer our lives to you this day, and our life together in you: all our words and deeds, all our hopes and fears, and our amazing love. Accept us as we are, with all our stumbling and with all our courage.
Guide us into what you would have us be. And in the power of the Spirit enable us to be a sign of your presence in the

world, after the pattern and in the name of Jesus, your true
and well Beloved. Amen.

*I think this is the best place in the ceremony to use either this
or another similar formal prayer, or, better, to say together a
prayer that you have written for this unique occasion. It might
even begin with each saying to the other what gifts he or she
hopes to bring to the relationship, and then conclude with a
joint prayer of offering.*

A prayer for the couple

Spirit of the living God, strengthen N and N that they may
persevere in love, grow in mutual understanding, and give to
each other in ever-deepening trust.
Shower them with your gifts of wisdom, patience and
courage, that their love may be a source of happiness, and
their home a place of welcome for all who are their guests.
We pray this for them with all our might, after the pattern of
Jesus and in the power of the Spirit.
Amen.

*Again, this is a prayer which can easily be adapted by using
words worked on by the couple themselves. How do you wish
to grow together? What are the gifts you need? What are your
hopes for your life together? Most of the words used here have
been said before in this order of service. There is room, therefore, for variety. But there is no harm in repetition. After all,
the language on such an occasion is the language of love, and
love's song is endlessly repeated. Say it again and again. I never
tire of hearing you say those words.*

A blessing

God the Giver of life, God the Bearer of pain, God the Maker
of love, bless, preserve and keep you.
The divine light illuminate you, and shine out even from
the cells of your being, guiding you in truth and peace and
making you strong in faith and wisdom, that you may grow
together in this life,
and with the love which endures, be carved and polished
like diamond, with the love that can never be overcome.
May it bear you even beyond death itself and transfigure you
to glory.
**God bless you both, as we bless you from our hearts, now
and always. So be it.
Amen.**

*The last three lines give something for everybody present to say
together. Blessings are shared among us as well as coming from
beyond what any one of us could do or say.*

An invitation to the witnesses

I give you N and N!
Applause
Will you, the chosen witnesses of their covenant this day, do
everything in your power to support and encourage them in
the years ahead, quietly being there for them in times of stress
and sorrow, with laughter being there for them in times of
celebration and joy?
We will.
God has called us in the spirit of friendship to live in peace.
Let us share with N and N and with one another a greeting of
peace. The Shalom of the living God be with you. The peace
of the loving God touch your heart.

A blessing for lovers

May you never step on each other's toes, lest the damage be worse than a pedicure can save!
May you always speak truth from the core of your souls, even when doing so seems risky and brave.
May you never fall asleep during episode six, lest the catch-up be long and the time be short.
May you always keep talking through good times and bad, to nurture your own special communication and rapport.
May you never stop living the magic of dates, from a weekend away to an hour behind closed doors.
May you always seek to discover more of what makes your lover smile, gasp or moan wanting more.
May you never lose sight of the marathon ahead, with God in the centre and your hopes well aligned.
May you always embrace the vitality of life, whether cishet, trans or queer, as God designed.

SUFFERING PRESENCE

There are some versions of Christian faith that see suffering as a sign of spiritual failure or being overcome with evil and therefore something we should strive to avoid. The truth is bitter-sweet. Suffering, turned aright, is perfectly normal and human and can also be formative and redemptive. Some of the most powerful kinds of witnessing we have encountered emerge out of suffering. The witness of faith in suffering is sacred and can be saintly. Even when the pain and loss is acute and grievous, it is the witness to faith and hope in the face of evil, and the light that will not be overcome by darkness, that testifies to God's eternal commitment to dwelling among us. Full of grace and truth; not repaying evil for evil; and meeting hate with love. In this section we offer resources for prayer and contemplation in the midst of suffering. We share in this together.

Protest

ELLA WHEELER WILCOX

This poem by American Ella Wheeler Wilcox (1850–1919),
written at the peak of the Women's Suffrage movement and
just as World War One was about to erupt, is a mighty and
mobilizing anthem against silence and stands as an anthem for
our own time.

To sin by silence, when we should protest,
Makes cowards out of men. The human race
Has climbed on protest. Had no voice been raised
Against injustice, ignorance, and lust,
The inquisition yet would serve the law,
And guillotines decide our least disputes.
The few who dare, must speak and speak again
To right the wrongs of many. Speech, thank God,
No vested power in this great day and land
Can gag or throttle. Press and voice may cry
Loud disapproval of existing ills;
May criticise oppression and condemn
The lawlessness of wealth-protecting laws
That let the children and child-bearers toil
To purchase ease for idle millionaires.

Therefore I do protest against the boast
Of independence in this mighty land.
Call no chain strong which holds one rusted link.
Call no land free, that holds one fettered slave.

Until the manacled slim wrists of babes
Are loosed to toss in childish sport and glee,
Until the mother bears no burden, save
The precious one beneath her heart, until
God's soil is rescued from the clutch of greed
And given back to labour, let no man
Call this the land of freedom.[1]

Notes

1 Ella Wheeler Wilcox, 'Protest', *Poems of Problems*, Chicago, IL: W. B. Conkey, 1914.

John the Baptist: St George's Church, Kingston, Jamaica

MARTYN PERCY

I recently came across a story about the first Bishop of Minnesota, Benjamin Whipple, who tells of an incident in his autobiography, *Lights and Shadows of a Long Episcopate*, of the Dakota Indians under the presidency of Abraham Lincoln. After being driven from their land, the Dakota tribe revolted and a large number of white settlers were killed in several days of massacre – mostly led by younger Indians, anxious to prove themselves.

The Dakota Indians were rounded up indiscriminately from their lands and 438 were condemned to death by hanging. The Indians appealed to Lincoln for clemency, saying that most of the incarcerated men were innocent, and indeed many of them had risked their lives by hiding white settlers from the marauding bands of young braves. Bishop Whipple tried to intervene for the innocent men, and Lincoln duly commuted 400 of the death sentences: only 38 Indians would die.

But which ones? The elders of the tribe – the oldest men – stepped forward. We have seen our children and our children's children, they argued. We have few winters left. We shall die in place of the young, who, even though they committed the raids and the massacres, have children to raise. The press reported the hangings and the newspapers in Washington said that the Indians went to their deaths 'singing their heathen death chants on the gallows'. But Bishop Whipple, who stood by the accused, records it differently. The ones executed were, you see, Christians – Indian converts. As Whipple tells us in his autobiography, they went to their death at Fort Mankato chanting Psalm 92 in English: 'Many and great are your works, O God; Many and great are your works, O God; Many and great are your works.'[1]

The connection between a sacrifice – one made by us or by someone we know – and the freedom of others, or ourselves, to flourish, is one, perhaps, we take for granted. The equation, however, is rooted in Scripture, and in the lives and ministries of both Jesus and John the Baptist.

So what has John the Baptist got to do with us? Sometimes it is uncomfortable to own the connections that bind us to one another. But this is a ministry of costly preparation. John the Baptist is not the main attraction, or the warm-up act. John the Baptist: without him there is no preparation for the Messiah. No John, no Jesus.

This is not as heretical as it may at first sound. After all, the Gospels make a virtue out of utilizing and subtly re-narrating the narrative from the book of Isaiah: 'Prepare ye the way of the Lord ... make way' is how it is expressed to us. Now, there are two senses of 'make way' here, and both are implied. One is clearly proactive, namely make *the* way: clear the path; make the rough places smooth; create the road.

But the other is more humbling: 'make way', as in 'get out of the way', because he is coming. Here, we are to step aside and take all obstacles, including ourselves, out of his path. For we are not the message or the messenger; the One who is to come is not to be obstructed.

Whichever way one reads the use of the passage from Isaiah by the synoptic writers, it is clear that for those who follow John the Baptist, the common denominator in the vocation is the ministry of preparation. For those of us who follow him, we are the seed, not the fruit; the cause, not the result; the start, not the finish; the beginning, not the end. We are those who prepare the way. So arguably, there cannot be a more apposite saint for Christians.

For here the ministry of preparation is life-giving. John's role is to prepare the ground; to make a way in the desert. On this, Jesus can come. But this is tough work.

John's work is not just a few speeches and a couple of short sermons. This is costly and hard ministry. It will marginalize John; and it will bring about his death. So, I imagine in some small way that Jesus' words in the Gospel of John give us a vital connection to the ministry of John the Baptist and that of Jesus. Significantly, the first three Gospels place these words of 'preparing the way' and roadbuilding in a context in which the road is wide open. There is a wonderful modern poem from Heather Pencavel, just called 'Roadbuilding':

Roadbuilding is rough work
hard labour, muscles strained
hands calloused, back near breaking
even with lifting gear, hard hat, protective boots.

Site clearance is dirty work
and dangerous
removing rotten structures,
risking unsafe ground,
uncovering long-forgotten corruption
– the stink too strong to breathe
of waste and dereliction.

God, you cry out to us
to clear the site, build the road
because you are coming
and you will come
along the road we build.

Give your people, we pray,
the will and stamina for the job.
Give us courage to tackle the clearance
of debt and exploitation
which corrupt communities and nations.
Give us the grit and determination

to straighten out the crooked structures
which make it hard for the poor and the weak
to journey to freedom.
And help us to shout aloud that you will come
along the road we build.
(© Heather Pencavel, Advent 2017)[2]

Yes, the prophecies of Isaiah all seem to be coming true. And
yet, it is already the case that 'unless a grain of wheat falls into
the ground and dies, it remains a single grain; but if it dies, it
bears much fruit'. We already know how John's story will end.
The connection here is one of paradox. Unless we step aside
– die to ourselves – we cannot bear fruit. We must yield ourselves, our power, ourselves – so that what God longs to give
birth to will be seeded, grow, flourish and mature.

This is no easy lesson, to be sure. But it is the only one we
have to ponder on as we learn from the example of John the
Baptist, where we prepare the way for the One who is to come.
I sometimes think that our role in life is to be more like John:
to own the ministry of preparation. It is John's willingness to
both make way and give way that we celebrate. His ministry
of preparation – a life of extraordinary sacrifice – in which the
connection between repentance and hope becomes realized.
Leonardo Boff, in his poem, tells us what we can expect from
such costly service:

History is usually told by the victors.
It is they who preserve the written documents,
erect monuments,
and have epics sung about themselves
in order to immortalize their deeds.
Who will tell the history of the vanquished, the losers?
...
All these people fell.
They are Jesus falling again and again
in the course of history's Way of the Cross.
Jesus is already risen from the dead,

already in the glory of his Father.
But his resurrection is not complete
because his passion still goes on
in the passion of his brothers and sisters.
...
It is to such people that God promised the kingdom.
And it is all the more theirs
insofar as they do not succumb to feelings of impotence,
insofar as they work to anticipate it by enacting
   profound changes
that create the real conditions for justice, peace,
   and reconciliation.
...
All memory of suffering awakens dangerous visions,
visions that are dangerous for those who try to control the
   present or the future.
They are visions of the kingdom of justice,
which enable the suffering people to shake off their bonds
and to keep moving along the road to liberation.[3]

And so John the Baptist prays one of the few short prayers that we as the followers of Christ will ever need: 'he must increase – and I must decrease'. John's testimony is simple: he is coming. John decreased, Christ increased. So, let us, with the Word made flesh, work with God to be a path and make some way in this needy world of ours - the one that Jesus came to redeem: make way.
   Amen.

Notes

1 See https://www.youtube.com/watch?v=Ll-2WEtb_40.

2 Heather Pencavel, 'Roadbuilding', in Geoffrey Duncan (ed.), *Shine on, Star of Bethlehem: A Worship Resource for Advent, Christmas and Epiphany*, London: Canterbury Press, 2004.

3 Leonardo Boff, *Way of the Cross – Way of Justice*, trans. John Drury, Eugene, OR; Wipf & Stock, 1982.

Solidarity and Struggle

MARTYN PERCY

Gavin Francis is a GP, and his recent book *Intensive Care* (2021) reflects on the nature of pandemics and how we respond. What I admired most about the book was his neat summing up of the skill that a GP needs for the role: 'science with kindness'. Not enough is written about kindness, yet it is an essential core element in most vocations and arguably most professions.

I used to remark to students at Cuddesdon that once they were ordained, most mistakes and faults would be forgivable. Bad preaching is not ideal, but it is tolerable. Poor administration is not helpful, but it is unlikely to be the deal-breaker between parson and parish.

That then begs the question, what is the deal-breaker? I would counsel seminarians about to be ordained that they must be one thing, at least, and this was non-negotiable. They had to be *good*. Yes, good. Good people, full of goodness, and ideally overflowing with the milk of human kindness. This meant that in being good, they must also be utterly truthful.

Truthful and good. That is what we need from our clergy, and it is not a bad thing in our GPs and others who work in caring professions and vocations. I'll take a good pastor any day, over and against an untruthful and bad person, even if they are someone who is a brilliant preacher, liturgist, administrator or leader. Goodness and truth matter most. Yes, most of all. Being good matters.

For the earliest churches, goodness and truth spilled over into the sharing of the good news. That good news was not a mere sermon, however. Good news meant actions, lifestyle, kindness and sharing. There was no good news for the poor if it just turned out to be a newsflash from a street preacher ranting about sin and salvation. Good news for the poor meant a good church and truthfully *feeding* the poor. And keeping them warm, in shelter, and treating them with dignity and kindness.

The goodness and truth at the heart of Christian faith is Jesus, the living bread. The shared meals and feeding those who could not feed themselves extended from the very heart of the Eucharist. Just as Jesus, the Living Bread, is for all, so was the church to be a community that fed and nurtured the widows, orphans and those who could no longer care for themselves, or whom society (or religion) had discarded.

As I have said, Bethlehem, where Jesus was born, means 'the House of Bread' in Aramaic. So, from the crib to the Last Supper, to Emmaus and to our altars, the bread we share is *banal* – common food, symbolic of spiritual and inward nourishment, that binds us together as one body.

Common food and common eating is the hallmark of fellowship. When training for ordination, Emma and I spent a year on placement at Consett in County Durham. This once proud steel town had been decimated by the economic ravages of Thatcherism, and rates of unemployment were high, with the other accompanying indices of poor health, obesity, smoking and long-term depression. Yet working with the curate and community there was a source of endless, utter joy. The congregation and parish were terrific company and moving exemplars of resilience and hope.

It is the leaven of the communal suppers and lunches that Emma and I often recall, over 30 years on. For the menu was always the same: corned beef pie. It was sometimes served cold, in 'slabs', or hot, with a side of boiled potatoes. We never quite got the hang of the recipe, but it was essentially corned beef mashed with potato and filling an 'envelope' of short-crust pastry. It is fair to say that as a meal it was filling. Indeed, I sometimes wondered, with the winds whipping off the moors, if the function of this food was partly ballast. The top layer of pastry was not latticed and it came as it came, hot or cold.

The appreciation for this local Consett fare lay in its

commonality. We all ate of one social meal, and it therefore bound us together, so there was no enmity or any kind of competition in the provision of food, of cooking skills, and so of class, taste or other particularities that might divide us. Corned-beef pie meant something: this is us – we share our social life, lot and fellowship together.

There is one body. One pie. Irrespective of education or occupation, or the lack of either or both, there was no room for any sneering snobbery when it came to food – what the sociologist David Morgan defined as 'a matter both of public disapproval and private enjoyment'.[1] All partook of one meal.

Years later, when Emma became vicar of a parish in Sheffield (Holy Trinity Millhouses), the common meal for the congregation was meat and potato pie and minted mushy peas. Again, you might think, more ballast than nutrition? Perhaps. But this common, repeated menu had a quasi-eucharistic function. This is how we expressed our life together socially, not just liturgically.

Like bread and wine each day, each week, the common meal for social occasions expressed our unity and our equality. Goodness and truth meant that we ate together as one, because we were committed to the goodness of unity.

So, pie was for sharing. Just as Swiss hamlets still remember and celebrate the community bread oven located in the centre of most hamlets or villages, with the loaves apportioned out as each person and household needs through the long winters. This work was regulated in each community by a 'Banal' – our word for 'common', but the Swiss term for the village council that looked after everyone, so fostering the common good.

My resolution for the Church is: be good, be truthful, and share with those who lack food, shelter and kindness. In feeding them, we feed Christ. This is our common task, and indeed should be our common prayer.

Notes

1 David Morgan, *Snobbery*, Bristol: Bristol University Press, 2018, p. 37.

Three Christmas Homilies

God's abiding and abode

Martyn Percy

Some years ago, a professor of psychology at the University of Louvain took an interest in how people feasted and celebrated. As part of his research, he asked one of his students to write a thesis on the following subject: 'How do children, aged 9–11 years, experience the phenomenon of *feast*?' The student approached the subject in various ways, and one of these consisted of showing a controlled group of 100 children three different drawings of a birthday feast.

In the first drawing, the picture depicted a child alone, but before a mountain of gifts and presents waiting to be opened. In the second drawing, the child was not alone, and was surrounded by just a few members of their family, and some food – a birthday cake, ice-cream and other treats. But there were many fewer presents to open – in fact only one parcel, and not a very big one at that. In the third picture, the child was surrounded by wider family, friends and neighbours, and there was more food. But there was no gift or parcel in the picture at all, so nothing to open.

The question the children were asked was simple enough: which of these birthday feasts would you rather have for yourself, and why? Seventy per cent of the sample chose the third picture.

So they explained, as children might, that this was the *real feast*. Others said, 'Because in the third picture, everyone is happy – in the first picture, only I am happy, and in the second picture, not enough people are happy.'

The children, in other words, grasped something authentic about celebrations. That by being together, and only by being together, can we be truly happy. A true feast, in Christian thinking, is a communion with God *and* a communion with people – the two are indivisible. So it is with Christmas. God bids us welcome – to a meal that is collective in character, because God's feasts are profoundly communal. Christmas is the Birthday Feast of Christ.

Perhaps, like me, you have despaired over the character of our political deliberations this past year (2016 – Brexit, President Trump, UK General Election ...). At times, our debates felt like an advocacy for the first two birthday pictures I described earlier. That we are somehow better off on our own, or with just a very few folk we know well and feel comfortable with. Yet the Christmas Birthday Feast of Jesus is inclusive by nature.

The early church understood this. So the first Christians looked after the widows, orphans and poor. And they treated them not as objects of charity but as their equals. They did this for foreigners, friends, neighbours, slaves, free, male, female, young and old. As John Chrysostom wrote, '*Ubi caritas gaudet, ibi est festivitas*': 'Where charity rejoices, there we have the feast'.

We will surely look back on this year, like any, as a Year of Shocks and Surprises. But every year throws up major challenges, such as migrants and asylum seekers fleeing the violence of Syria and other countries, in a desperate bid for their lives.

So what is there to hope for? 'The Gate of the Year' is the popular name given to a poem by Minnie Louise Haskins. King George VI quoted the poem in his 1939 Christmas broadcast in the early days of World War Two. You'll know these lines:

I said to the man who stood at the gate of the year:
'Give me a light that I may tread safely into the unknown.'
And he replied: 'Go out into the darkness and put your
hand into the Hand of God.

That shall be to you better than light and safer than
a known way.'
So I went forth, and finding the Hand of God, trod gladly
into the night.

So what of us as we contemplate taking our first steps into the
coming new year? The Gospel of John speaks of light in the
darkness and of God 'abiding' with us. The word links to
the English word 'abode'.

God, in Christ, comes to dwell with us. If we dwell in him,
he will abide in us. He bids us to make our home with him, as
he has made his home with us. God is Emmanuel – God is with
us. Even when it may all seem dark and hopeless, the light of
the world has come.

Some of you will know that a fortnight ago we lost Emma's
brother to cancer. Chaz was 49 and had been living with
Emma and me for several months, as he could no longer live
independently. We were ably supported by staff here and, in
the last week of his life, by Sobell House. But in between my
brother-in-law coming to live with us and his end, part of my
fortnightly routine had been to take him to the doctor's, and
also do the weekly run to the pharmacy for the morphine and
other drugs.

So after Chaz had passed away, I went back to the pharmacy
with a card and some chocolates, and a very large quantity
of unused drugs that could have sold very well on the black
market. The gifts were a simple 'thank you' to Anna and
Alison, the two pharmacists who had worked so hard on the
docket boxes of medication and patiently measured out each
day's drugs: fiddly, mundane work that requires concentration
and precision. But they had always done it with such cheer-
fulness, and on the days I had taken Chaz with me, they were
always so good to him too.

So I plonked my shopping bag of drugs on the countertop of
the pharmacy, conveyed our thanks for all they had done, and
handed over the chocolates. We chatted for a while, and I was
about to take my leave when they said, 'Wait there, please –

don't move.' And then they came out from behind the counter and warmly embraced me, in a tender, deep hug of knowing and consoling. So there the three of us embraced in the middle of Boswell's pharmacy. We must have made quite a sight; a most unusual trinity. And in a real sense, that is what Christmas is. God leaves his station and comes round to our side of the counter. He does not stand apart from us – remaining aloof, as it were, measuring out love and grace behind a distant counter. No. God enters the world from our side and embraces us here, in our pain and loss. He knows our losses; he consoles us. He is Emmanuel, God with us.

I had lost my beloved brother-in-law, and here, in this failing, frail, tired flesh of mine, two women held me as Christ might have done. Surely, he has borne our griefs and sorrows. Because he has taken on our flesh, and lived among us, and fully as one of us. And loved us in that flesh, and loves us in eternity. This is the meaning of the incarnation. God has come to our side of the counter. And so we encounter him as one of us. God has entered our nature; joined life from our side. Emmanuel. Come: let us give thanks for and share in this Christmas feast. The light of the world has dawned. Amen.

It's the economy, Stupid

Martyn Percy

The proper countdown to Christmas begins early, as it does every year. The Feast of the Annunciation, 25 March, celebrates the moment when Mary says 'yes' to God and immediately conceives. Yet unlike most pregnancies, planned or otherwise, our Lord spends precisely nine months in gestation. Not a day more; not a day less.

In classic Christian thinking, it is normal to see the infant Jesus as the saviour-in-waiting. Apart from the complicated business of actually growing up, Jesus' path and destiny are already marked out. The more spiritually alert folk – his mother, the wise men, Simeon, Anna and the shepherds – all seem to know what is happening. Salvation is coming through this one child.

And yet the Gospels give us a much more subtle picture to attend to. The bringing of salvation to the world, beginning in Bethlehem, turns out to be a work in which the cost is surprisingly shared out among many, not just left on the shoulders of one tiny infant. Mary must say 'yes': the annunciation is her sacrifice. Jesus escapes the wrath of Herod, but thousands of infants do not – they and their parents pay a heavy price for the coming of the Christ-child. Others, such as John the Baptist, lose their lives for Jesus before he can sacrifice his. God's salvation incurs debts.

The bearing of grace, then – God's Riches At Christ's Expense, as the Sunday school mnemonic goes – is not actually quite right. Salvation, even one wholly initiated by God in Christ, costs other people too. In bringing heaven to earth, Jesus' is not the only sacrifice. In short, God cannot do it alone; Mary's 'yes' is needed, right the way through to the unknown helpers on the refugee trail to reach the asylum of Egypt.

Indeed, many of the characters in the Christmas stories are studies in Christian virtue, discipline and generosity. The innkeeper offers hospitality when he is stretched and his hotel bursting at the seams. Yet somehow he manages to extend his boundaries to find one more room – to be inclusive – so that nobody is ultimately debarred. Very like the ministry of Jesus; very like the mansions of God. There is room.

The wise men bring strange and extravagant gifts, speaking of the foolish generosity so rarely found in monarchical power, but especially bestowed in God's. The shepherds mirror the spontaneity and searching of Christ – you may find him, but he will come looking for you anyway. And the people of Egypt, too often unsung, support and sustain the unlikely asylum seekers in the shape and form of the holy family. The gospel crosses all borders and boundaries; but Jesus the refugee is first received in a foreign land. Small wonder, then, that as an adult Christ will preach on the importance of welcoming the stranger.

So, looking at salvation in terms of God alone bearing the cost is by no means ideal. The reason why the Sunday school mnemonic, with its emphasis on 'expense', may be a distortion of the Christmas story is that it implies some kind of penalty – Jesus pays the price which should have been ours. While that is one way of interpreting the gospel stories and the New Testament, it isn't the only way of reading our tradition.

I think that the Christmas salvation story itself is far richer. Grace should really be seen as something that is expansive as it is expensive. God involves many people in that work 'of gathering up all things in Christ' and allows all sorts of folk to participate in his saving work. You are not just in debt, needing to be 'bought out of bondage'. You are also a partner in this extraordinary work.

As anyone who has ever had a child will tell you, a tiny inarticulate infant is utterly absorbing and demanding. And God has come among us as a tiny child. As John says, 'He came into the world, but the world knew him not; but to those who received him and believed in him, he *adopted* them as his own' (author's translation). So yes, in adopting this child here and now, God then adopts us for eternity. A famous prayer catches this wisdom for the Christmas season:

> Blessed art thou, O Christmas Christ, that thy cradle was so low that shepherds, poorest and simplest of earthly folk, could yet kneel beside it and look level-eyed into the face of God.

So yes, God's riches come to us at Christ's expense. God's welfare state is free to all. Don't worry about the cost. Christ has paid. Receive first, and then slowly learn to believe. The cost of this economy is unbelievable. But always free.

God makes himself at home with us

Martyn Percy

Here is one of the better jokes pulled from a Christmas cracker last year. Good King Wenceslas rings up his local pizzeria. 'I'd like a pizza delivered, please.' 'Will that be the usual order, sir?' says the voice on the other end. 'Yes,' says Wenceslas, 'deep pan, crisp and even.'

Or consider these 'classics', drawn from the BBC's Top Ten 'Christmas Cracker' jokes. Did you hear about the two ships that collided at sea? One was carrying red paint and the other was carrying blue paint. All the sailors ended up being marooned. Or, what did the grape say when the elephant stepped on it? Nothing. It just let out a little wine. Or, why did the man get the sack from the orange juice factory? Because he couldn't concentrate. I am sure you can do better ...

To most people, Christmas comes as both a panic and a relief. Some of us go to great lengths to plan it in every conceivable detail. But many things will happen unplanned! Rather like preparing for the birth of your own child, you have a schedule and strategy. But then it just happens. It's a bit like football or war. All the tactics are fine and dandy, until the game starts or battle commences. War and football tend to get complicated when encountering the opposition. Christmas gets complicated when encountering reality – or perhaps just family who come to stay. As I say, it is *so much* like a birth.

So what is Christmas all about? Well, this is 'the House of Christ' – a place where the founders of this cathedral, college and institution, which we know simply as Christ Church, determined that God himself would find a home. Indeed, home is part of the meaning of Christmas. He has made his home among us. He came to us, and as one of us, and has dwelt with us. He has lived among us, shared our lives, and lived through joy and agony, pain and death, humiliation and celebration. He is Emmanuel: God with us; God among us; God living with us.

In the exquisite novel *The Boy in the Striped Pyjamas* (2006) by the Irish writer John Boyne, and the no less beautiful retelling of the story in Max Herman's film of the same name (2008), we encounter eight-year-old Bruno and his family leaving Berlin, during World War Two, to take up residence near the concentration camp where his father has just become commandant. Unhappy and lonely, Bruno wanders out behind his house one day and finds Shmuel – a boy in striped pyjamas who lives behind the barbed-wire fence, about a kilometre away from the commandant's house.

The boys become friends – an unlikely friendship, indeed – and play games through the wire. Eventually, the German boy, Bruno, finds a way of getting inside the camp to be with his friend. But in order to really fit in, he asks to put on the striped pyjamas worn by Shmuel and all the other inmates. Shmuel finds him a spare set and passes them through the fence to Bruno. Bruno quickly dresses like Shmuel and sneaks into the camp. Before they go back to the hut, Shmuel asks, 'Are you sure about this ... are you sure you want to do this?' Bruno replies, 'There is no place I'd rather be, and no one I'd rather be with.'

I won't spoil the ending of the book or the film, but I think you may guess how things end for any eight-year-old in striped pyjamas in a concentration camp. But this little scene is all you really need to know about Christmas. For God, in the ministry of Jesus, says: 'There is no place I'd rather be, and no one I'd rather be with than you.'

Christmas is God making his home with us. Not just here, in the House of Christ. But home, with you. Christmas is God saying to you: 'There is no place I'd rather be, and no one I'd rather be with.' Because, in his Son, he sends us a simple message at Christmas: he is crackers about us. Crackers enough to live, love and die for us. Crackers enough to dwell here, in this, 'the House of Christ'. Crackers enough to be completely at home with you, in your home. Christmas is simply this. This may be the House of Christ, *Aedes Christi*; but he is at home with you, enjoying you and loving you more than you can ever, ever comprehend. God is born into a home so he may always be at home with you now; and so you can enjoy a home with him for eternity.

Mary Needed Room

EMMA PERCY

Mary needed room;
room to be noisy.
To cry out in pain.
To groan in labour.
To curse the angel and her God.

Mary needed room;
room to be messy.
For waters to break.
For blood sweat and tears.
For her body to follow its natural urges.

Mary needed room;
room to be apart.
Away from the noisy crowd.
Away from the gaze of men.
A place for women's work and women's wisdom.

And in that room,
in the noisy, messy, women's work of labour,
a child is born,
Hope is delivered
and the Light came into the world.

A Prayer in Suffering

THE ORDINARY OFFICE

I can't. I can't do this any more.
I feel you, God, as close as the blood in my veins yet I can't
bear what you ask of me.
You ask, 'Open your eyes, Child.'
I can't. Not today.
My body is weary, the pain is too much. My heart is heavy
and if I open my eyes, the tears will just flow. And flow.
And flow.
You say, 'Open your eyes, Child.'
I can't! Hear me!
Here I can rest with you, hide in safety, you will keep me
from harm. We can dance over all the unfamiliar words filled
with joy your Spirit gives me, as you call me the name only
you do. I can take inspiration, be fortified, be nourished.
I can feel free.
You whisper, 'Open your eyes, Child.'
I get it now. Thank you, sweet Yeshua. My pain is my pain.
Yet you are here within it. You give me your words to take
out into the world, so there can be a little more joy and a
little less pain. In love and for love. I will do it.
Thank you, God, for opening my eyes.

A Service for Racism Sunday

THE ORDINARY OFFICE

Introduction

Racial Justice Sunday is an ecumenical observance which began in 1995 in Britain and Ireland. The catalyst for this observation came about in the wake of the murder of Stephen Lawrence, a young black teenager in South London, on 22 April 1993. In 2017, Racial Justice Sunday moved from September to the second Sunday of February. This service is for congregations, chaplaincies, churches and others. It represents a call for Christians to witness to and engage with the righteous struggle for racial justice – because racial justice is a concern for each and every one of us. The gospel calls all Christians continually to witness against the evils of our world and to proclaim justice and mercy as we seek to walk with our God (Micah 6.8).

Gathering prayer

God, we come before you today with much to lay down and much to ponder. We have seen such violence, yet such love. We have seen such discrimination, yet the start of real resistance. We have seen such fear in the face of restrictions lifting while others rejoice. Holy Spirit, we welcome you into the heart of everything we are feeling. Move us in the direction Jesus would move. Direct us to walk the steps Jesus would walk. Guide us in the actions Jesus would have us take. Above all, loving God, help us to keep our eyes on you, so we may always know your peace. **Amen.**

Welcome

Welcome again to this sacred place, this holy ground, as real to us as any church building. Our home is here on YouTube, on Twitter, on Facebook and on our website. Online is where we live and have our being. These are places of welcome, open to all. Stay for as little or as long as you like, be as involved or not as you feel comfortable being.

Many of us that gather here were unable to access physical church even before there was a pandemic, and here we have been made welcome and found a home; this is our space. Come on in and join us.

We dedicate this space to those who may feel they have little to look forward to, to those who feel they have nothing to contribute, to those who have been made to feel unworthy, and today especially to those who worry about what the future of church, or their faith, may look like for them.

Father, take this place, and those gathered here, and make this a place of hope and encouragement, a place of refuge, a place of peace.

To those who are new here, we say, welcome.

To those who are excited to be here, we say, welcome.

To those who don't know why they are here at all, we say, welcome.

To those whose seeking led them here, we say, welcome.

To those who feel like they have always been here, we say, welcome.

To those who have faced discrimination, fear and abuse, we stand with you against such things and we say, welcome.

To those who dare to hope, and for those who dare not hope yet, you are welcome.

To those who join us at a later time or date, you are welcome.

Above all, Jesus, we welcome you into our presence.

All this is your temple, Lord. Although there are no walls, the web is where we gather. As real to us as any church. Computers, phones and tablets are our prayer books. Our prayers float in the ether like incense across the sanctuary. Fellowship comes in many forms, and ours is here, online.

Confession

Let us take a few moments to consider the times when we have not acted as we would have liked this week.

All: For the times we have not been able to keep our manners, or our tempers, we say, God, forgive us.
For the times we have not been able to understand, or seek understanding, we say, God, forgive us.
For the times we have not recognized or challenged our inherent prejudices, we say, God, forgive us.
For the times we have not done as much as we could have to support our neighbours and communities, we say, God, forgive us.
For the times we have not cared for ourselves in the midst of this pandemic as well as we could have, we say, God, forgive us.
In asking your forgiveness, gracious God, help us to be transformed, that we might live as people of your kingdom, following your way and trusting your wise counsel.
Unite us with those who stare through the window longing to be allowed in.
Unite us with those alone in their grief.
Open our hearts, Lord, to the warmth of your love.
Amen.

Statement of community

Though we are far apart, let us feel a closeness.
Let us reach out across the ether.
Unite us across time and space.
Teach us to be alone yet together.
Though we are socially distant and in isolation,
let us feel your touch,
the warmth of your love enfolding us.

Prayers

God, as we listen to your call to oppose injustice, challenge
oppression and stand for what is just, we take a moment to
give thanks for the things that keep us going in times of need.
For this space where we can express our emotions in safety,
we thank you.
For a service we are able to attend easily, we thank you.
For friends amid the darkness, we thank you.
For people who understand, we thank you.
For a place where we feel safe, we thank you.
God of light, a light that breaks through the darkness.
A light that penetrates all hidden corners.
A light that comes to us through a little child, born in Bethlehem.
We have followed your star and it has brought us here.
May we continue to diligently search for him each day,
so that we may offer our lives to you in joy and thanksgiving.
Teach us a new song, Lord,
a song for those who go unsung.
Praise the ones that do our dirty work:
the pushers of chairs, the wipers of bums, the makers of tea,
the givers of meds.
Teach us that new song, Lord, that lets them know they
are loved.
The ones who put their own dreams on hold, Lord, who give
until they are spent.

The ones who go unnoticed, Lord, quietly meeting our needs,
yet keep us rolling along.
Teach us to say thank you, Lord, for every ounce of care.
God, let us now bring before you those we know of in need of
you at this time. In a moment of silence, we hold them before
you and ask you for your blessing on their lives.
Those who cannot see, he walks with as guide.
He whispers softly to those who cannot hear.
He soothes those whose minds are troubled.
He rides with those who cannot walk.
He sees the pain of those whose pain cannot be seen
and brings insight to those who appear not to understand.
God of hope, bring us love that dwells between us.
God of hope, who brought peace into this world, be the peace
that dwells between us.
God of hope, who brought joy into this world, be the joy that
dwells between us.

Reading

Revelation 7.9–10

Sermon

Response

Those gathered are invited to nominate someone to come forward and light a candle, and pray in quiet for:

- Those who have lost their lives through slavery – historic
  and modern.
- Those who have been unfairly judged and executed because
  of the colour of their skin.
- Those who face discrimination today because of their ethnicity.

- Those who are persecuted in the long march for justice and equality.
- Those who campaign for unity, diversity, fairness and parity.
- Those who are made fully in the image of God, yet treated as inferior because of their ethnicity, heritage or identity.

The person leading the service can invite the congregation to say 'Amen' after a short silence for all those we remember and give thanks for.

Blessing

Even as you face injustice, know that God is just.
Even as you face unfairness, know that God is fair.
Even as you face discrimination, know that God does
not discriminate.
For Jesus walked with the poor, the weak, the oppressed, the exiled, and he walks with you today.
And may the peace that comes with the knowledge of that love reside with you today and always, by the Spirit left with us, in Jesus' name. Amen.

A Service for Bereaved Parents at Home Preparing to Lay Their Child to Rest

THE ORDINARY OFFICE

We begin this service by lighting this candle in remembrance of a child who is loved and as a reminder that God is our light in the darkness of sorrow.

The candle is lit with the following words
Loving God, as we gather in memory of this special child,
your mysterious silence and presence touches us.
We hold before you and each other the hopes and dreams that we held,
as we thank you for the gift of this short life.
Words cannot express all that we feel at this time; be with us as we give expression to the pain of grief shared as we say goodbye. We ask you to bless this candle. May it signify the love and memory in which this child is held and be a light of hope for the future.

Readings for reflection

'The LORD called me before I was born, while I was in my mother's womb he named me ... I will not forget you. See, I have inscribed you on the palms of my hands.' (Isaiah 49.1, 15–16)

'[The LORD says,] "Do not fear, for I have redeemed you; I have called you by name, you are mine ... you are precious in my sight, and honoured, and I love you".' (Isaiah 43.1, 4)

The sign of the cross

God says: 'Before I formed you in the womb, I knew you.'
And we remember that Jesus welcomed little children, took them in his arms and blessed them.
For *N*, Jesus lived.
For *N*, Jesus died.
For *N*, Jesus rose again.
He has welcomed *N* into his eternal kingdom.
Therefore, as a mark of that love and grace, we place on *her* the sign of the cross. *N*, Christ claims you for his own. Receive the sign of his cross. God has delivered us from the dominion of darkness and has given us a place with the saints in light. *N* received the light of Christ.
Let us pray: God of love, we thank you for the assurance of your presence. Help us to trust in the promises you have made. Surround *N*'s parents, their family and friends, with your love and grace. Comfort them in their sorrow and fill them with your peace. Strengthen their faith in you and bless them with confidence and courage to face the future, through Jesus Christ our Lord.
Amen.
God of compassion, help us to believe that *N* is in your gentle care through the grace of our Lord Jesus Christ.
Amen.

Our Father,
who art in heaven,
hallowed be thy name,
thy kingdom come, thy will be done;
on earth as it is in heaven.

Give us this day our daily bread.
And forgive us our trespasses,
as we forgive those who trespass against us.
And lead us not into temptation, but deliver us from evil.
For thine is the kingdom, the power and the glory,
for ever and ever.
Amen.

Go gently on your voyage beloved,
slip away with the ebb tide.
Rejoice in the new sunrise.
May the moon make a path across the sea for you.
May the sun provide a welcome.
May the earth receive you and the fire cleanse you,
as you go from our love into the presence of love's
completeness.

Blessing

May the God who walks beside you, reach out and take
your hand.
May you hear God's loving voice and feel God's gentle touch.
May God fill you with peace and comfort you in the presence
of the Holy Spirit.
May every tear you shed, every word you share and every
memory you treasure bring you deeper healing.
In all these ways, may the blessing of God hold you close, day
by day.
And the blessing of God Almighty, Father, Son and Holy
Spirit be upon you and remain with you always.
Amen.

Suffering in Silence

EMMA PERCY

When they ask you how you are
should you reply with platitudes:
   bearing up
   not too bad
   surviving,

or risk exposure

stripping off your clothing
to show weeping wounds
barely healed scars
simmering anger
a vulnerable child.

If you do
many will turn away in embarrassed distaste,
murmuring self-justifying denials of complicity
and an assurance of prayers
as they hurry to cross the road.

Few, but oh so precious,
are the ones who lift you onto their donkey
and lead you gently to the inn.

When You are Ground Down

EMMA PERCY

When you are ground down
by the burden of life
the trespasses of others
the casual indifference
and the calculated disdain
   – take hope.

Grounded you can choose
to become humble.
Brought low you can choose
to become meek.
Lowly you can find
you are blessed.

Through grace you can begin
to build from the ground up
to root deep in the soil
to build foundations and plant fruit.

You can laugh at the pomposity of their palaces
knowing that when the storm comes
foundations matter
and the meek shall inherit the earth
the humble shall see their God.

Stretch

EMMA PERCY

Muscles ache, tired from over and under use,
pulled out of shape by long habits of tension.

The invitation is to stretch,
to relax into an open posture
to allow the loving presence of God
to touch and release.
And yet I resist – tense up.
Help me to trust that in letting go
I will not fall too far,
that in opening up
I will not be violated,
that in stretching myself
I might in the end find
freedom of movement,
freedom of spirit, joy and pleasure.
    Teach me to stretch.

Suspension

EMMA PERCY

Removing the baubles from the tree I note the thin cotton
thread by which they are suspended,
so fragile, breakable.
Looking across into the hall I see the forged chain from which
the central light hangs
and I think about our suspension:
how it leaves us hanging, vulnerable, exposed.
The ground has been taken from beneath our feet.
There is the possibility of a fall from grace,
and yet we are held.
The chain which holds us is forged from fine precious metal.
It is woven together from the love of our friends.
Strengthened by the prayers of so many.
Shot through with the faithfulness of God.
It is made out of kindness and integrity
shaped by years of hospitality and hopefulness.
And we are grateful for such strength.
Mindful of such graciousness.
Resilient in the face of adversity.
We look up not down trusting that somehow this time
will pass.

Blessed are the Meek

EMMA PERCY

Thank heavens for gentle folk,
The meek and the good.

Who treat others with love and kindness
Who welcome all with open-mindedness
Who hold lightly to this world's wealth
Who cultivate their spirit's health
Who know how to listen and when to speak
Whose meekness is strength; humble not weak
Who lighten our load and rejoice in what's right
Whose generous souls bring us all into light
Who are blessed by God and proclaimed of great worth
These, gentle and faithful, will inherit the earth.

Limbo

EMMA PERCY

Recently I have spent a long time in limbo.
My fate is in others' hands.
Timetables shift and concrete information is in short supply.

It is a heavy place;
the burden of uncertainty and the needful alertness
leave little respite from the agony of waiting.

I am a bit player in this drama.
Caught up in the banal cruelties of power games
I am not entitled to play.

I see the fallout, the broken relationships,
the dogged inability of some to admit error
or seek a path of forgiveness.

In the midst of the clouds
rays of kindness break through giving me hope.
There is a promise I cling to that this, too, will pass.

Yet, for now I plough on through the fog,
waiting for a change in the weather,
hoping, above all, that I will not have lost my way.

Blessed are the Peacemakers

EMMA PERCY

We all want to be peacemakers
reconcilers, bearers of hope.
Yet, we gloss over the cost.
Peace-making, peace-planting
is hard work.
Heavy lifting is needed for ground clearance.
Diplomacy for de-cluttering.
There will be anger as you
remove false idols from pedestals
and violence as you name
injustice and dismantle walls.
For peace to flourish,
rights of way must be reclaimed,
level playing fields constructed,
fortified borders breached,
barricades torn down,
swords turned into ploughshares,
privileges laid aside
and differences embraced.
To do this work,
to commit to this labour,
requires a pure heart
and a confident faith.
Blessed are the peacemakers
for they are the children of God.

Breathe

EMMA PERCY

  – Breathe
Breathing is always good
Slow, steady
  – Pause
Take time in responding
Calm, measured
  – Speak
Carefully choose the words
Truth, honesty.

Anger needs to be tempered
for righteousness' sake.
Indignation tested
for self-understanding.
Courage found to stand your ground,
for words matter.

Some things need to be said
Some voices need to be heard
Some certainties need to be challenged.

So breathe, pause, and speak.

Fig Leaves

EMMA PERCY

To have one's eyes opened
To be confronted with the inconvenient truth
And to see the consequences
Of the comforting assumptions
Leaves us uncomfortable
Exposed, vulnerable
And ashamed of our nakedness.

No wonder time and again
We practise the absurdity
Of sewing fig leaves into loin cloths
To cover our shame
And, if we have the power,
Conscripting acolytes
To praise the glory
Of our invisible clothes.

Prayers in the Midst of Domestic Violence

This prayer was written in the current climate of increased awareness and discussion about violence against women, intimate and domestic violence cases.

Loving God, in recognition that there are those for whom believing in their relationship over warnings, caution or reputation does not work out well, we take a moment to reflect and pray.

For those who have entered into relationships or interactions in good faith, and have been abused in mind, body or spirit, we pray.

Send your Holy Spirit upon them now, and give them peace. May they know the sweet, gentle rest that comes only through being in your presence.

For those whose circumstances enabled them to make the decision to tell someone, report, share their pain and be heard, we thank you and ask for peace. We pray for justice, that in telling stories change will be brought and society will change through one brave person at a time.

For those whose circumstances meant this could not happen, we thank you that you walk by the side of each and every individual, loving them and offering your comfort, as you always will. That you will guide them towards healthy ways to process their trauma, and caring people to support them as they do.

For those who have been able to tell someone or report in later times, we thank you and ask for resilience. Give them strength and perseverance when the road becomes tough, determination when dead ends and road bumps appear, and the wisdom to know in their own hearts where their own journey for resolution must take them. Walk by their side in each and every step towards healing, loving God.

May we strive to be a society that listens and hears. Where the silencing which hallmarks abuse can be immediately lifted through reporting. Where safeguarding processes work and reporting processes bring justice. Where victims have confidence their privacy is respected and perpetrators know they will be appropriately held to account.

Above all, may we be known as people representing places of safety and care. Where we grapple with these complex issues with a heart of humility. Lead us, loving God, to always do the right thing. May the paths we walk and the words we speak encourage others to do the same. Help us listen, hear, learn, repent, do better, be better. As Jesus called us to.

Peace be with us all. Amen.

What do we do, when peace is so fleeting, and conflict so rife around us?

Look to the sky. See the soft, rolling clouds and watch the gentle movement of the earth. On and on it turns, in a constant, life-giving path. Know it turns to give you the sunlight you need, and the darkness to rest. That is how much God loves you.

Look to the earth. See the green shoots, abundant in the country or persevering through the cracks in urban space. On and on they grow, in a constant, life-giving effort. Know they grow to give you the air you need, and to clean the air in turn. That is how much God loves you.

Look to your heart. See the space within where the Spirit lives, rests and resides in you. On and on they work, in a constant, life-giving endeavour. Know they are there, purifying, pruning, gently weaving the strings of your heart together with their own in a beautiful braid. That is how much God loves you.

Feel the peace that comes with the knowledge and understanding that this is how much God loves you.

Amen. Peace be with you.

Prayers for Pride Month

THE ORDINARY OFFICE

Everyone is awesome.

Triune God, whose very essence is mystery, fluid, relational. We thank you for all of the varied and beautiful ways this is expressed in our humanity.

For those who stand proud with their loved one, in same-sex union of any kind. We thank you for the steps towards wider acceptance, and we ask you for continued progress to be made. For Love is your greatest commandment, over all.

For those who are unsure of who they should love, what gender they are, how their internal personhood matches who they were assigned to be at birth. We thank you that awareness is better and help is available, and we ask for continued progress to be made. For Love is your greatest commandment, over all.

For those who have cisgender, heterosexual privilege afforded to them by societal norms, let them use it wisely to help their marginalized siblings up, not hold them down. We thank you for strong, vocal allies throughout society, faith groups and communities and we ask for continued progress to be made. For Love is your greatest commandment, over all.

Where biblical translations of rhetorical devices and ambiguous wordings may lead to unfair marginalization of your queer children, God, may we always remember the absolutely clear direction to Love Thy Neighbour. For if we love, how can we judge and harm?

Amen.

Peace be with You.

Like a gull soars over the ocean, roaming watchfully, may your gaze soar over us.

Like a dolphin plays gracefully in the waves, dancing lightly, may your Spirit dance with us.

Like a child watching the sand trickle through their fingers, gasping in awe, may we always stand in awe of you.

Like a crab scuttling to find the perfect shell, seeking hopefully, may we always find a home in you.

Like a seal basking on the rocks, resting peacefully, may we always find a place to rest with you.

Wherever our situation, whatever our experience, however we find you, God. Draw us always to find you.

Amen.

Peace be with you.

DEATH AND RESURRECTION

There can be no resurrection without a death. Still, it is only human to try and cling to what we have and hold, and find it unbearable to let go. Death, as Woody Allen once said, is nature's way of slowing you down. Death reminds us that graveyards are full of indispensable people with unfulfilled commitments and urgent appointments. But death comes to us all, and we cannot know the liberation of new life, hope and resurrection unless we can hold on to our lives as a gift. A gift that one day must be given up, returned or offered for someone else. We are always on borrowed time. Yet in the gift of resurrection we are reminded that it is at the point when we lose life for God's sake, we find it. Just as Jesus found in the tomb early on Easter morning. In this final section, we explore through prayers, blessings, liturgies, poems and homilies what it means to accept death in order to receive life. In that journey, may God be with you, and with us all, always.

Ripening

EMMA PERCY

For ripening there must be
   The plant and the soil
   The sun and the rain
   The insects to pollinate
   The careful cultivation of
   Pruning and nurturing.
Seasons must come and go
   From buds to flowers
   From fruit to seeds
   The dead wood of winter
   The new shoots of spring.

Humbled

EMMA PERCY

When you are brought low
When you are humbled
When you are ground down
And hit rock bottom
Humble yourself
Feel the solidity of the earth
Become grounded

Then when you know who you are
Hold firm to the rock
Feel its strength
Clamber up
And find your feet.
Raise your head and
Carefully, tentatively
Walk forward
With a new perspective
A new understanding
A new joy in living.

The Sign of Jonah

Readings: Jonah 1 and 2 Peter 3.14–end

MARTYN PERCY

One of my favourite Woody Allen lines is this: 'If you want to make God laugh, tell him your future plans.' The story of Jonah is hardly a barrel of laughs, but for anyone with a vocation it ought at least to raise a wry smile. For Jonah has a sense of purpose and is indeed dedicated to it. And yet, he suspects that not all will go according to plan, almost from the outset. The story is one that teases us with the sheer fickleness of God's grand plan and the total inadequacy of our own plans. Packed with prayers, petitions, it begs more questions than it can ever answer.

Jonah is my favourite book in the Scriptures, and not only because it is short, but because of its utter profundity. It has four chapters, several prayers, a rather improbable storyline, and is the only book in the whole canon of Scripture to end with an explicit question to both its reader and subject. The question, put in modern idiom, is God speaking: 'Why should I not be concerned?' And the question ends, tantalizingly, with the line 'and many cattle'. God, it seems, is even bothered with the beef herds.

Jonah son of Amittai is a prophet from Gath-Hepher (a few miles north of Nazareth), active during the reign of Jeroboam II (*c.* 786–746 BC), where he predicts that Jeroboam will recover certain lost territories. Jonah is also the central character in the book. Ordered by God to go to the city of Nineveh to prophesy against it, 'for their great wickedness is come up before me'. Jonah seeks instead to flee from 'the presence of the LORD' by going to Jaffa and sailing to Tarshish. A huge storm arises and the sailors, realizing this is no ordinary storm, cast lots and learn that Jonah is to blame. Jonah admits this and states that if he is thrown overboard the storm will cease.

This is all very well, but the sailors still try to get the ship to the shore; failing, they feel forced to throw him overboard, at which point the sea calms. Jonah is miraculously saved by being swallowed by a large fish, specially prepared by God, where he spends three days and three nights (Jonah 1.17). In chapter 2, while in the great fish, Jonah prays to God in his affliction and commits to thanksgiving. God commands the fish to vomit Jonah out.

God again orders Jonah to visit Nineveh and to prophesy to its inhabitants. This time he goes and enters the city crying, 'In forty days Nineveh shall be overthrown.' The people of Nineveh believe his word and proclaim a fast. The King of Nineveh puts on sackcloth and sits in ashes, making a proclamation to decree fasting, sackcloth, prayer and repentance. God sees their works and spares the city at that time.

Displeased by this, Jonah refers to his earlier flight to Tarshish while asserting that, since God is merciful, it was inevitable that God would turn from the threatened calamities. He then leaves the city and makes himself a shelter, waiting to see whether or not the city will be destroyed.

God causes a plant (in Hebrew a *kikayon*) to grow over Jonah's shelter to give him some shade from the sun. Later, God causes a worm to bite the plant's root and it withers. Jonah, now being exposed to the full force of the sun, becomes faint and desires that God take him out of the world. But God says to him, 'Are you really so very angry about the little plant?' (or 'The good is what you are angry at!' according to a traditional Jewish translation).

You are concerned about the bush, for which you did not labour and which you did not grow; it came into being in a night and perished in a night. And should I not be concerned about Nineveh, that great city, in which there are more than a hundred and twenty thousand people who do not know their right hand from their left, and also many animals? (Jonah 4.9–11)

Jonah, like most of us, is a reluctant follower. He is reluctant to go to Nineveh because he suspects all along that God hasn't got the bottle to carry out the threats he, Jonah, is supposed to warn them of. Jonah suspects God is soft. He thinks that the Ninevites will say sorry, God will say OK, and that will be that. And he's right. So Jonah quits before he's begun. And that is where the story begins. He goes down into the belly of the ship, where his rebellion festers and gestates. He is taken to the belly of the whale through the storm and learns what Paul Murray calls 'the pregnant lesson' of God.

Jonah has chosen not to listen to God; he hides in the womb of sleep and the womb of the ship – safe from the storm and safe from God's call. But from this womb of rebellion, Jonah is sucked in deeper into the darkness and chaos of the sea, and of the giant fish. But here Jonah does not die. He lives in the darkness and is eventually spewed out through the very jaws of death on to dry land. Jonah's prayer is from the belly of the whale – the waters swirl around and he is trapped. It is from there he calls to God.

There is an important lesson for us here, just in the first half of the book. According to the philosopher John MacMurray, there is a critical difference between good religion and bad religion. Bad religion says: 'Trust in God, pray to God and fear not, and God will see that none of the things you fear will happen to you.' Yet good, or mature religion says something different: 'Trust in God, pray to God and fear not – the things you most fear probably will happen to you, but they are nothing to be afraid of.'

The difference is explored at length in the book of Jonah. Most of what Jonah fears happens. But the book is about learning to live with that, and not resenting God for God's will being done. God spares Nineveh. God raises a plant; God sends a worm to destroy it. He spares the cattle. Don't complain. Learn to live with it. The lesson for our time could hardly be more pertinent. Indeed, it comes up in our epistle from 2 Peter 3 – patience and fortitude are required; stay faithful.

Over the years, I have realized that as a reluctant theologian, occasional dissenter and cage-rattler, and as a priest, I identify strongly with Jonah. And I wonder if you do too? It would be much easier to say 'no'. But as you know, all evil needs to flourish is for good people to do nothing. Do something; not anything; but try and make sure you do the right thing. But we are all human, and sometimes it is easier to withdraw and refuse the conflict. Modern lives prefer shortcuts and making alternative travel plans.

The prayer lesson of Jonah is not about petitioning God for what we want. It is, rather, being honest before God about who we are and what we hope for. It is about waiting in the belly of the whale, in the deep. It is about patience, pregnancy, gestation. Prayer is a slow, patient business, in which our wills are entwined and desires changed as our spirituality deepens.

In one of the darker moments over these last few years, and when all had seemed very bleak to me, Emma wrote this poem. She's been writing very fine, perfectly publishable poetry for a few years now, since the loss of Chaz, her younger brother. This one is called 'Another Economy', and it rejoices in the good that might be found in the midst of all the crap, for want of a better turn of phrase.

I have found that there is a different economy
Whose currency is
Love and kindness
Faithfulness and prayer
Generosity and integrity.
When these virtues are practised
Deposits are made and investments accrued.
So, when the world turns harsh
And desolation beckons,

I find I am rich.
And I can draw on this wealth
Providing me with
Friendship and kindness
Prayers and blessings
Fortitude and strength.

So, stay strong; stay faithful; have courage, and foster your fortitude. Remember that in the huge storm that Jonah encountered, and the several that Jesus knew on the Lake of Galilee, you are never lost, nor ever abandoned. God sees you. God is with us. 'Do not be afraid' and 'Do not fear' are phrases repeated a great deal by Jesus in the Gospels – more than 70 times, in fact. We would be wise to remember that 'perfect love casts out fear' (1 John 4.18), yet also remember that the reverse is also true: 'perfect fear drives out love'. Our calling as Christ's followers is not to be fretful and fearful, but rather to become an extension of God's courageous, endlessly expended love for this world. Our calling does not seek its own security, or indeed reward. It is to express the continual love and risk revealed in the incarnation; to become like Jesus, who is the body language of God.

Chaz

EMMA PERCY

People ask 'Where do the dead go?'
'Is there life beyond this life?'
We could have a discussion about:
heaven and eternity
bodies and souls
life everlasting,
but that is not for now.
Now, I simply want to say
that in this time of trial
my brother, who left this life,
full of faith and hope, some three years ago,
has been present with me
in ways I cannot begin to explain;
and his presence has been a comfort.

A Prayer for Easter

THE ORDINARY OFFICE

Thank you, Lord, for your daughters. The ones who came to serve Jesus when no one else would. The ones who gave their best oils for the one they loved. The ones who grieved wholeheartedly, for what was asked of them was beyond understanding.

Thank you for your children who give all they can to serve you.

Thank you, Lord, for your daughters. The ones who rushed to tell the world about Jesus at a time when their word meant less than male slaves. Evangelists who risked everything to bring incomplete truths to a shattered, broken community. The ones determined to do the right thing, whatever the cost.

Thank you for your children who give all they can to serve you.

Thank you, God, for your daughters. The ones who called your sons to witness and brought them to your tomb. The ones with the strength and conviction to secure belief in the unbelievable, to draw them from their stupor and deliver hope. The ones who reignited the spark of your followers, giving rise to the flame of our faith.

Thank you for your children who give all they can to serve you.

May we commit ourselves afresh to you this Easter, to serve you as your daughters did.

Coming Through Fire:
Notes on Connections between
Daniel and Jesus

Daniel 6.1–23 and Luke 24.1–9, 36–43 and 50–53

MARTYN PERCY

I must confess that, following our Old Testament reading, I feel a bit like a lion in a den of Daniels. Let us hope I fare as well as the original Daniel did. But in all seriousness, if we were to have a Bible quiz on what connects our two readings, I'd be awarding points and prizes for the following observations (in the C+ to B++ mark range).

First, both Daniel and Jesus are placed in stone-sealed tombs and written off as dead. Second, both are victims of plots and betrayals. They are spied on, too. Their persecutors are motivated by malice and malfeasance, and they mean to harm. Third, Daniel and Jesus are both tried and convicted in a manner that is unfair and denies them justice. Fourth, both cheat death ... quite miraculously. Daniel defies death – the lions don't harm him. Jesus does endure suffering and death, but is resurrected. Fifth, their survival or resurrection confounds their witnesses and puts the judgement back on the persecutors. Sixth, they reverse their prosecution and persecution, not by acts of vengeance but by gracious, holy example. Seventh, as a famous Dean once said, 'Only the gentle are truly strong.' He was right, and this is true of both Jesus and Daniel, post-trial and post-tribulation. Incidentally, the Dean in this quote above was James Dean – so not a cleric!

Yet what is the deeper connection within these passages? Can I suggest three links that you might not notice at first sight, but they are there in the texts.

First, and in the case of Daniel, he is, like his compatriots, Shadrach, Meschach and Abednego (see Daniel 3 – they come through fire!), a eunuch. Jesus, as you may recall, was quite pro-eunuchs. In fact, he thought they made quite good disciples. Here is what Jesus says in Matthew 19.12:

> For there are eunuchs who have been so from birth, and there are eunuchs who have been made eunuchs by others, and there are eunuchs who have made themselves eunuchs for the sake of the kingdom of heaven. Let anyone accept this who can.

Jesus, like many people 2,000 years ago, regarded eunuchs as reliable, dedicated and dependable – ideal discipleship. Jesus regarded the lack of offspring as a potential source of blessing – not being tied down with family, or the cumbersome business of burying their recently deceased father. Or joining the disciples only after attending to family matters; nor pausing to complete an important livestock investment, property deal and land purchase, before signing up for service.

Eunuchs have existed since our earliest histories and were generally deemed to be reliable. That word 'reliable' might seem a rather odd term for us to pay much regard to in our day and age. Modernity is essentially an age of reliability. As eunuchs had neither offspring nor in-laws and were invariably made to be eunuchs from a relatively young age, they were groomed to be trustworthy. They were programmed to undertake certain tasks. Eunuchs formed a powerful group in the Roman Empire. They served the imperial bedchamber, privy to the innermost workings of the Empire. Our word 'eunuch' comes from the Greek for 'bed-guard'.

However, let us tackle that unavoidable technical question: eunuch – but how? Essentially, there were four different types.

Spado (plural: *spadones*) was the generic term for asexual men, who may have been born without strong sexual characteristics. So, without the full sex organs or those whose sex organs failed to develop at puberty.

Then there were *thlibiae* – those whose testicles had been deliberately bruised or pressed. The Greek verb *thlibein* means 'to press hard' and the process here was to tie the scrotum tightly in order to sever the *vas deferens* without amputation. The genitals would therefore appear normal. Another type were *thladiae* (from a Greek verb *thlan*, 'to crush') where the testicles were crushed between two bricks, rendering the person (or victim) sterile. Finally, there were *castrati*, undergoing a partial or full removal of their sex organs. This was done to pre-pubescent boys to produce catamites.

Please note, these procedures are not requirements for entry into the Civil Service or Foreign Office today. However, please also note that eunuchs were the earliest practitioners of 'safe sex'. As one ancient writer put it with great diplomatic delicacy, eunuchs permitted one to 'savour the blossoming flowers of passion, but without being burdened by the fruit of such unions …'.

So my first link between Jesus and Daniel relates to their status – foreigner and yet also close advisor to the king in the case of Daniel, and in Jesus' case he is the rabbi-teacher-political-social-activist and also well disposed to foreigners. Both are set apart for this and considered to be a danger and threat to the prevailing powers. Their vocation is not much picked up as thrust upon them, and because of that their bodies must suffer for this.

Second, and linked to this, with the recent recovery of African American histories, Christians are coming to terms with collusion in privileging white-male normativity. You may never have seen a copy of the *Slave Bible*, specifically published for educating slaves in the early nineteenth century. Its full title was *Select Parts of the Holy Bible for the use of the Negro Slaves in the British West-India Islands*. Such Bibles had all references to freedom and escape from slavery excised, while passages encouraging obedience and submission were emphasized.

It was a kind of racist *Reader's Digest* version of Scripture – where the editors served up just 10 per cent of the Old Testament and around half of the New Testament. Excluded passages were Galatians 3.28 ('There is neither Jew nor Greek, there is neither bond nor free ...'), which was thought to have potential for inciting rebellion. Passages such as Ephesians 6.5 ('Servants, be obedient to them that are your masters according to the flesh, with fear and trembling, in singleness of your heart, as unto Christ') were retained.

The targeting, sexual abuse, deliberate humiliation and physical emasculation of criminalized or deliberately demonized black men in the early twentieth-century Deep South often involved tarring and feathering, preceding their castration, before eventual lynching. This was set out as a spectacle before the prurient curiosity of large crowds of white spectators, and it is well chronicled. You could even buy souvenir postcards of such events (which many witnesses did), mailing (goading?) their 'friends' living in liberal eastern US states.

We might remember that many of those targeted to die were condemned before they could be tried and judged, even though it was to be an all-white-male jury. I think of the words uttered before Jesus in the court of Caiaphas: 'Why do we still need witnesses?' (Matthew 26.65). Jesus was condemned to death before the defence or prosecution had presented their case. Why bother with justice? That was Daniel's experience too.

Jesus was stripped, whipped, scourged and mocked. You may find his silence eloquent, powerful or puzzling. Yet I think in our age, his silence echoes differently and cries across 2,000 years of sexual, marital, emotional and physical abuses. The #MeToo and #ChurchToo movements remind us that victims are often forced into silence. As many victims of sexual violence testify, it was by becoming passive and no longer resisting that the ordeal was over quicker, and the violence lesser. Some victims also believe they may die quicker, and less painfully, if they do not struggle or scream. There is no point in protesting or resisting the groups of men hitting the blindfolded Jesus; striking, beating, spitting at, taunting and abusing him. The perpetrators kept their identity anonymous; their victim was in the dark.

Recently discovered first-hand accounts of Roman crucifixions reveal that the victim might be forced to watch their family or friends brutalized, beaten or raped. The disciples had good reasons to be scarce at the foot of the cross. Getting caught up in a crucifixion – as a friend or family member of the victim – was an extremely dangerous business for witnesses. Ancient shame culture was the deliberate stripping of a person's dignity and honour. Victims of crucifixion were often pinned up naked, with their slow death through asphyxiation producing its own perverse spectacle. Unable to exercise any self-control of their muscles or reflexes in their body, this sadistic cruelty only added to their public humiliation.

Third, one of the early lesser-known Christian heresies was from Eutyches, who taught that Jesus' ascension was a spiritual event, not a physical one. The heresy was attractive 2,000 years ago, even without the aid of complex telescopes, as few wished to ponder the thought of Jesus flying past Mars and turning right at Venus before taking a hard left at Saturn. Modern cosmologists like the late Carl Sagan pointed out that if Jesus was ascending at the speed of light, our most powerful telescopes would still be able to see him. The erstwhile liberal American bishop, Jack Spong, used to say that Sagan's observation showed how daft the doctrine of the ascension is.

I profoundly disagree. The ascension … spiritual, physical, symbolic … does it matter? Yes, it does, and hugely. As the early church father Origen said, when Jesus returned to his Father, the angels at the gates of heaven were startled, and almost denied Jesus' admission or entry, because the angels reasoned that 'the corporeal shall not pass into the incorporeal'. But Christian orthodoxy says this must be so. Because Jesus bodily ascends to his Father with his wounds in his post-resurrection body. Why does this matter?

Jesus returns to heaven with our humanity, and his. If you believe in Jesus' bodily incarnation – as I do – then his ascension must also be bodily. I can explain neither biologically nor cosmologically. But theologically, humanly and spiritually, this obviously really matters. What is not assumed is not redeemed. If true of the incarnation, death and resurrection, it is also true of the ascension.

God does not now dispense with the flesh, heartache, suffering and frailty of humanity. It is returned to the Father in the person of Jesus, where it remains abiding in God: until he, Jesus, comes again in glory (Matthew 16.27). As Hebrews 7.25 says, 'He is able for all time to save those who approach God through him, since he always lives to make intercession for them.' Jesus continues to be incarnate, and our humanity abides in the love of this divinity.

So Daniel and Jesus emerge from their ordeals of fire. Not only intact, but also vindicated. Daniel's miraculous survival, and Jesus' resurrection, are a judgement on their accusers and abusers. As Romans 8 says:

Who will separate us from the love of Christ? Will hardship, or distress, or persecution, or famine, or nakedness, or peril, or sword? As it is written,
　'For your sake we are being killed all day long;
　　we are accounted as sheep to be slaughtered.'
No, in all these things we are more than conquerors through him who loved us. For I am convinced that neither death, nor life, nor angels, nor rulers, nor things present, nor things to come, nor powers, nor height, nor depth, nor anything else in all creation, will be able to separate us from the love of God in Christ Jesus our Lord. (Romans 8.35–39)

Nothing can separate us from the love of God. Or, for that matter, our persecutors. Daniel and Jesus emerging from their tombs affirms this for us all.

I know that we all have our own experiences of profound betrayal, and sometimes treachery. I know too that we wait and hope for justice, and that we should work for that. But we also worship a God of infinite grace, mercy, forgiveness and love, and this is sometimes too hard for us to bear. I put it to you that what binds Daniel and Jesus together is their trust in God and their refusal to seek vengeance. They come through their ordeal, not seeking to return blow for blow, or injury for injury, but with a different call to us. It is not one that sanctifies passivity or preaches cheap grace. There must be justice. But it must flow from truth, mercy and love.

So, for the one who reaches out to the despised and rejected, God says, through Christ, that he too will know something of that rejection. The scripting and patterning of this in the life of Jesus is as important for the story of salvation as is the cross. You have to see it as a whole. Sometimes the rejection is active, and sometimes quite passive. But Jesus is sensate to both; this is integral to God's incarnation: the word became flesh. God knows precisely what it is to be human. This includes our deepest pains, which are often not only imprinted on the body but also in the soul and heart. Some years ago, there was a competition on Radio 4 to write a short sermon. The winner was called 'The Kiss', and it went like this:

'Good to have you home, Son. Sorry you were in so much pain.'
'It wasn't the nails that hurt, Dad. It was the kiss.'

Our attention is drawn here to the deeply physical act of kissing. The kissing of Jesus' feet by an unknown woman; the kiss of Judas in betrayal. But whatever kind of kiss it was, the point is simple. God dwelt with us, among and as one of us: the word made flesh. And it is that flesh that returns to heaven in the ascension. Even flesh marked by pain, torment and torture. The flesh that Jesus returns to heaven with is every bit like ours. It has been loved, held, embraced and cherished. But it is also weathered, aged, beaten, betrayed, rejected, despised and defeated. It must labour to be born, and it must struggle and gasp for breath at the very end of life. Finally, it has died. This is the flesh of the resurrection too. The one still marked with nails, but now raised. Amen.

The Anointing Woman

EMMA PERCY

The woman sees Jesus and she takes
the jar of perfume oil, which she breaks
over his head or perhaps his feet,
while, embarrassed, others sit and eat.
An anointing, an ordination,
a consecration and preparation.
She is a prophet and penitent
proclaiming Jesus as heaven sent.
Her one holy act of foolish love
in which she mirrors her God above.
Whose generous love will be outpoured
in the sacrifice of Christ our Lord.

A Prayer for the Resurrected Church

THE ORDINARY OFFICE

Almighty God, Lord of All.

As you humbled yourself to death on a cross, to be resurrected into something new, may your Church find the strength to do the same.

May we humbly leave all traditions born out of mistranslation, human prejudice and political agendas at the cross, and leave the tomb with inclusive, grace-filled and welcoming approaches to kin-dom building, in Jesus' name.

May we humbly leave all hierarchies built out of a need for control, power and careerism at the cross, and leave the tomb with open, facilitative, lay and clergy partnership approaches to kin-dom building, in Jesus' name.

May we humbly leave all riches, trappings of status and symbols of authority at the cross, and leave the tomb as priests to one another, siblings in Christ, showing the Holy Spirit as members of one holistic church community, kin-dom building in Jesus' name.

May all differences, theological, traditional or otherwise, be laid aside in the pursuit of love. A passion for your people which transcends all else, even death, as you showed us on the cross.

Amen.

Kingfisher

EMMA PERCY

We have walked this walk so many times
In and out of season
In all types of weather.

We have talked this talk too many times
Reasoning the unreasonable
Unpicking all the knots.

Today our attention is caught
    a glimpse of iridescent blue
We stop, the Kingfisher also stops
Perching momentarily on a branch.
Then, all too soon, he is off
And though we look
he is gone from our sight.

We take this as a gift and a sign
A reminder of halcyon days
A promise that they will come again
A glimpse of glory, elusive as the truth we seek.

Walking on we find that our own blues are lightened
by the colour of the kingfisher
our burden slightly lifted by this moment of beauty.
We are glad that, despite everything, we still have the ability
to lose ourselves, however briefly,
in the wonder of creation.

There Were Also Women ... (Mark 15.40)

EMMA PERCY

When I was eight, we moved. My parents' marriage had ended and my sisters, brother and I moved from the country to the edge of London with my dad. We were brought up in a loving but rather haphazard fashion. This meant a new church and a new school. At this new school, Miss Spencely and Mr Adlam, who took the assembly, would suddenly ask us to recite the 12 disciples – Simon Peter, Andrew his brother, James the son of Zebedee, John his brother ... I knew some of these characters from Sunday school where I had learnt Bible stories – Abraham, Isaac, Jacob and Esau arguing about soup, Moses in the bulrushes, Joseph's Technicolor coat and even some of the less well known, Gideon, Naaman the Syrian, Elijah in his chariot, and of course those male disciples. There were women – wives and mothers – and women whom Jesus met and healed, but they were rarely centre stage and not many were named.

At church, the vicar and the curate were men; the choir was for men and boys. However, I learnt that missionaries could be women. We prayed for our missionaries, Jenny in Afghanistan and Pat in Sudan – sometimes they visited and spoke about their work. For the young girl that I was, the message seemed clear; the one role for me to serve God was as a missionary.

When I was 17, a young teacher joined our church. For some reason she convinced the vicar that he should let her preach. I was captivated: perhaps I could be a preacher? At university

I attended a church with a deaconess. Jane preached and led services. She was a gifted preacher and pastor and the sense of vocation crystallized for me – this was my calling. So I shared this with my Christian friends only to be met with stern rebuffs – women should not preach!

Women should not be leading services in the church, hadn't I read my Bible? Jesus called men – Simon Peter, Andrew, his brother ...

So with the help of Jane, I went back to the Bible and I found that, yes, there were plenty of men but there were also women – some I knew, Mary Magdalene, Mary of Bethany and Martha (the busy one) but others I did not know, Mary the mother of James, Salome, Joanna.

These women, we are told, had been with Jesus in Galilee, came with him to Jerusalem, supported him out of their own resources, watched by the cross, went with the body to the tomb and witnessed the resurrection on Easter Day.

They were disciples, proclaimers of the resurrection, yet their names had not got into my list.

And I found other women, the women in the Old Testament, whose stories and names seemed to be missed out of my Sunday school and church education: Deborah the judge, Huldah the prophet; Shiphrah and Puah, the midwives who saved the male Israelite babies, including Moses.

And in the early church I found Lydia and Tabitha, Prisca and Phoebe, Mary, Junia, Lois and Julia. Women who hosted churches, worked as deacons, and were even numbered by Paul among the apostles.

These were women whose ministry was valued, who, despite the fact that history is written by the men, remained in the pages of Scripture. Yet they were barely spoken of in the churches where I grew up.

And as I explored further, I learnt about the saints (Hilda, Ebba, Catherine of Sienna). Why, I wondered, did James the Less, about whom we know little, get a saint's day but Martha did not? She was not only busy but was one of the first to recognize Jesus as the Messiah. Why did many translations call

Phoebe a servant instead of a deacon, because her name was a woman's?

And so with my newly discovered biblical foremothers and inspirational saints, I found the confidence to offer myself in the service of God and the Church and was duly trained, ordained as a deacon and eventually a priest.

Increasingly, there have also been women in the clergy – we have been both a gift to the Church and a problem. Welcomed by many, but there are those who still remind us that Jesus called Simon Peter, Andrew his brother ...

As I have continued in my ministry and become a mother, whose kids are now grown up, I have reflected more about what we have to offer from our experience of being women.

Genesis 1.27 reminds us that both women and men are made in the image of God. What can we learn as men and women about God in whose image women have been made? And again, going back to the Bible, I found language and images I could play with – the experience of birthing a child is offered as an image of change, transition, struggle and hope. Paul uses the image of a breastfeeding mother to talk about his ministry.

So I have played. I have allowed myself to listen to and read Bible stories from my perspective. Feeding the 5,000 became an interesting reflection on breastfeeding, enough to satisfy the needs of those who are hungry with more for the next day. I found others have gone before me. Bernard of Clairvaux used breastfeeding imagery to think about his role as an abbot, both Anselm and Julian of Norwich reflected on Jesus as a mother.

I reflected on the powerful imagery in Isaiah 49 of how God's love is like that of a mother who cannot forget her children, and I wondered why no one shared such verses with me as a child coping with a mother who had left me.

I continue to explore the biblical stories of women and the imagery about God, learning more about what it is to be a woman made in God's image and called into God's service.

So what is my hope?

My hope is that we will remember that there were also women. We will remember that among the community that travelled with Jesus and supported his earthly ministry there were women; some were individuals who were healed, like Mary Magdalene, others were women of substance and resources. There were a number of different Marys; there were Martha, Joanna, Salome and others. I hope that we will tell the stories of our faith, acknowledging these women and the other women named or unnamed who are there in the Scriptures. Moses in the bulrushes survived due to the faithful actions of midwives, his mother, his sister, Pharaoh's daughter – women of faith, women of agency.

I hope that we will hear the courageous and uncomfortable stories of women in the Bible like Tamar and Dinah, Jael and Deborah, Vashti and Esther. We will note that Paul includes the ministry of women in his addresses to the early church. We will remember the female saints as more than virgin or wife and mother, but as teachers, leaders and philanthropists.

And we will expect to learn about God from women's experience of the world, as well as men's. For there *were* also women, and women as well as men are made in the image of God.

It is 45 years since I sat in the assembly hall and recited the 12 disciples. It has been a journey of discovery learning that God loves women and that God works through women and that women are good enough for God – gift not problem.

Easter Hope

EMMA PERCY

Mary Magdala carried the perfumed oil
And Susanna the basket of sweet smelling herbs.
The younger women brought the water and the fresh linen.
We gathered in the darkness and followed the lantern light
    towards the garden.
We spoke only of practicalities.
It was too soon to speak of Friday.
The pain too much, the grief too raw.
We had seen death before
But not like that and not him.
It was Joanna who mentioned the stone
And for a moment we stopped,
Wondering if this trip were folly.
It had felt so right to be doing something
To be respecting his body, performing one last act of love.
Mary Magdala, always the confident one, urged us on.
There would be a way, this was a good thing we were doing.
The sun was rising and the garden when we arrived was
    bathed with dawn light.
I am not sure who saw it first.
The stone that had nearly stopped us, rolled away from
    the entrance.
We hurried forward, eager now to do what we had come to do,
Armed with our gifts of frankincense and myrrh.
But no body was there
The grave clothes neatly folded

And then one whom I can only describe as an angel speaking
    to us.
He is not here, he is risen, he is not dead, he is alive
And our feet taking us swiftly back the way we had come to
    tell the others
He is not gone, he is not dead, he is alive.

Bursting Our Minds

MARTYN PERCY

Just before I went to university to read theology, a friend gave me the American author Josh McDowell's book, *Evidence that Demands a Verdict* (1981), which claimed to 'prove' that Jesus had risen from the dead. I was assured that no matter what my lecturers said, 'This book would help to keep me on the straight and narrow.' My friend added that so long as I clung to the truth that Jesus was really alive, I would be able to count myself a 'true' Christian.

More than 30 years on, I can still number myself among the saints. But I have long since abandoned the idea that the Gospels' accounts of the resurrection constitute 'proof' in McDowell's sense. This is not to say that I think that the resurrection stories are analogical or parabolic. They may be; but I also believe they are attempts to proclaim something about real events that burst through every conceivable intellectual and world-view paradigm. Put another way, the words of the Gospels cannot ever do justice to the reality of the resurrection. The first Easter is simply more than tongues can tell.

But there is also a case for saying that the point of Easter is not so much the rolled-away stone as the carried-away Church. Those who want to 'prove' the testimonies as 'facts' have missed something important. The point of Easter is not about attracting punters to peer inside the empty tomb and persuading them as to the reasons why it is empty. It is about finding and encountering the risen Jesus in the very present.

So, the Easter story is not about proving beyond reasonable doubt that Jesus, who was dead, is now alive. It is, rather, an attempt to show that the 'Jesus project', apparently doomed within the ashes of Good Friday, is somehow born out of the indescribable experiences of the Sunday. To modify a Swedish proverb, good theology is 'poetry plus, not science minus'.

Thank goodness, then, that the Gospels do not end by giving us abstract doctrinal reflections to explain the resurrection. It is a matter of faith, which is why the stories – for all their raggedness, fear, passion and wonder – are the best vehicles Christians have for trying to narrate the first Easter. The advantage of stories is that they give us a kind of deep knowledge that abstract reasoning cannot provide. 'Story knowledge' is also about particularity and exactness – giving us real people doing actual things: going to anoint a body; running from the empty tomb; not recognizing the gardener.

The craving for 'proof', which is bound up with a flawed religious desire to make matters of faith into matters of fact, is as understandable as it is immature. But the need for certainty is not the same as the quest for faith. And Easter reminds us of the power of stories and the comparative weakness of dogma.

This is because rationality tends to evade the messy particularities of life, pressing on instead to deal directly with the generalized concepts that might lie behind the particulars. As Daniel Taylor remarks, such an approach often strip-mines reality, washing away tons of seemingly useless details to get to the small golden nuggets of truth. But the truth is in the details, in those vignettes that tell us of wonder, surprise and fear.

The Easter stories, then, are all we have. But they are enough. Never mind that Mark ends by saying that the disciples ran away, or that John records another story that none of the other writers seem to know about. The truth lies in the gaps. The point is that none of these narratives could ever have captured the ultimacy of Jesus on that first Easter Sunday.

But the stories do provide us with clues as to what to expect from the one who was dead but is now raised. A story of stark absence becomes a story of intense presence. The reality of Jesus is bigger than reality itself. But this is not evidence that demands a verdict. It is a faith, and a new life that invites a response.

New Beginnings

MARTYN PERCY

Resurrections are disruptive affairs. They confound rather than confirm, leading to that confusing cocktail of emotions, fear and hope. They sweep away order and reason, leaving the witnesses with no vocabulary and bedraggled by an event that is beyond reality.

As Christians celebrate Easter, the starkness of Lent yields to the sounds of celebration; the cry is 'He is risen' and acclamations of 'Alleluia' ring out from bell towers and congregations of every hue.

But the first Easter was an altogether more confusing and circumspect affair. The Gospels tell us that at the sight of the empty tomb, the disciples fled in fear. And as the appearances of Jesus increased over the following weeks, there were still doubts, questions and more fear. The resurrection broke the world in which the disciples lived, but the new order to which they were beckoned was, as yet, opaque.

In recent years, theologians, bishops and church leaders have found themselves in difficulties affirming what the resurrection is, and what it might mean. For some, the litmus test of orthodoxy has to be a literal affirmation in the historicity of the physical resurrection of Jesus. Anything less is deemed to be dangerous and heterodox. For others, the Gospel accounts can only be the best that language could do to convey an event that was, almost by definition, beyond words.

Yet for all sorts of theological reasons, the resurrection stories are important material to wrestle with. To be sure, the

Gospels affirm that Jesus, once dead, is now alive – but he has, at the same time, become an elusive figure. Sometimes present, often absent; sometimes easily recognized, sometimes appearing as a stranger.

Jesus' resurrection provides consolation and mystery in equal measure. In their resurrection accounts, the Gospels seem to be saying something about the very nature of God – that God cannot be pinned down. Recently, a bishop told his diocese that the most perfect image we have of God is Jesus hanging on the cross. Arguably, the plethora of crucifixes in our churches and our culture testifies to the popularity of that sentiment. But can there be a more perfect image of God to behold?

The answer from Easter Sunday to the question posed by Good Friday is an emphatic 'yes'. The most perfect image we have of God is an empty tomb; there is nothing to see, save a few linen cloths on a grave slab. The perfection of this image lies in the very absence of anything to glimpse.

Then there are those two emotions that the resurrection stories evoke: the fear of God (which is the beginning of wisdom), and completely unmerited hope. So the resurrection stories are packed with paradox, not persuasion. It seems that God's style is not to give proof but to pose questions. We are left with clues, not conclusions. The grave clothes are folded neatly, and yet the endings of the Gospels are untidy and ragged, as though God could not bear to say 'The End'.

The resurrection stories play with the borders and boundaries of our sense of reality. One minute Jesus cannot be touched (his very instructions to the weeping Mary); the next, he is to be touched (his command to Thomas). And in the middle of this quite human yearning for certainty, Christians are reminded that their religion is, ultimately, a faith, not a science.

So the Easter message is this. The tomb is empty. But there is no point in standing guard outside it, or trying to draw people's attention to the places where Jesus has once been – an empty grave will win few converts. And that is really the point of the Easter story. In the oldest account of the resurrection (by

Mark) and in the earliest Greek manuscripts, the Gospel ends mid-sentence, with the innocuous Greek word *gar* (meaning 'for': they were afraid for).

Thus, a proper conclusion to the story is withheld and it is up to the reader to say what happens next. The followers of Jesus are invited to write a resurrection conclusion with their own lives.

Candle

EMMA PERCY

So I lit a candle
the match struck on rough paper
producing a flame
a burning.
The element of fire
transferred to the tiny wick
tempered by the wax
into a steady light.

A tiny act of defiance
in the dark space
a symbol of hope
and prayer.
A controlled burning
for the purpose of illumination
to lighten and enlighten
the surrounding darkness.

Make me like a candle
that the fire of my anger
may be steadied to become
a source of enlightenment.
To guide the lost
to comfort the lonely
to defy the darkness
and banish the fear.

Resurrection – Group Exercises?

MARTYN PERCY

I am in a group exercise session at Diocesan Church House, on a training day …! So I naturally thought of you, the congregation gathered here today. Actually, it's not a bad day. Confirming, no doubt, that I've finally succumbed to a kind of ecclesiastical Stockhausen syndrome. Bishop Patty Hearst led the opening prayers in my dream last night, so my subconscious was already at work. I should have guessed. I came with hope. Christians are hard-wired for hope. There is no cure.

The table in front of me has lists of labelled cards that have to be correctly arranged by the group. There are no marks for pretty patterns. This is a linear exercise. I am feeling two things. First, when will the SAS come? I know we're in Oxford, but I'm near a canal on an industrial estate, so can't I call the coastguard?

Second, this is eerily like NCT classes, when all the men were taken to one side and given a diagram of the female anatomy, and some card labels. And asked to put the right card by the right bit of anatomy. As usual with group exercises, I retreat quietly to the back and observe, only participating towards the end. (No opportunity for ethnography should ever be wasted.) My reflection at our NCT was that if my male colleagues really thought those card labels actually corresponded to those anatomical drawings, it was a small miracle that any of the women were ever pregnant at all. ('Really? You think that is where that is …?')

According to the Gospel of John, Jesus' visit on the Feast

of Lights was the last trip that he made to Jerusalem before his own sacrifice. The next visit would be Christ's last, when he would return there for his final Passover and sacrifice. It is about reclaiming the purity of sacrifice; redeeming defilement.

Behold, this is the Lamb Who Shall Be Slain. A Shepherd and Sheep for slaughter. Christian tradition portrays Jesus as the Saviour, and in so doing reaches back to the Jewish perception of the Passover, of scapegoating and of the Pascal lamb. Here, in this death, and by the shedding of this blood, God will redeem his people. To be the victor, you must first of all be the victim.

So the Feast of the Passover is a bittersweet affair – and literally: bitter herbs, sweet meat. And at the feast, it is traditional to spill some of the wine as a reminder that the cup of joy is not filled to the brim, let alone overflowing. There are, in other words, more sacrifices to be made.

The joy of Easter, for Christians, must be tempered by the knowledge that the extraordinary life that bursts from the tomb does not just result in personal salvation for all who receive it. The resurrection, like the Passover, places responsibility on the community of the redeemed – to reach out to the alien and the stranger who also want to feast with us.

While the feasting of the first Passovers was only for those who are initiated into the faith of the Old Testament, Easter reminds us that the salvation that comes through Jesus is to be altogether more universal in the New Testament. In Jesus, the boundaries between us – native and alien, family and stranger, kith and kin – are dissolved. Jesus asks us to make our meals inclusive – as it shall be in the kingdom that is to come. So Christ our Passover is sacrificed for us. Let us keep this feast. But it is a feast to which the whole world is invited.

Easter Futures

MARTYN PERCY

On Easter Sunday 2020, the Archbishop of Canterbury was interviewed for the BBC's *Andrew Marr Show*. Inevitably, as the country was in lockdown, the pandemic dominated the discussion. I was especially taken by this comment from Archbishop Justin:

> Once this epidemic is conquered, we cannot be content to go back to what was before as if all was normal ... there needs to be a resurrection of our common life, a new normal, something that links to the old but is different and more beautiful.

Easter is a season that says that the world as we know it is turned upside down. Death has no more dominion. There is resurrection and new life. The old order has gone; behold, a new order is born. That is what Christians first believed and they had every reason to: they experienced the confounding of their old common life. Instead of cherishing the memory of a dead charismatic Galilean preacher and healer, they were faced with something wholly other: a resurrection commanding and creating a new social and moral order. This is Christianity: not simply a personal relationship with Jesus, but a commitment to living our communal life utterly differently from what went before.

From the beginning, Christianity was a tactile – yes, even a touching – faith. This new religious movement looked after widows and orphans. It gathered to break bread. It was congregational and social. It redistributed wealth and gave alms.

In this rather amusing depiction of Jesus and Mary Magdalene, we see the iconic rendering of John 21.17 in Fra Angelico's fresco adapted for the pandemic. It is ironic that 'Noli me tangere' has been inverted like this, because, of course, the resurrection is the fulfilment of the incarnation. In Christ, there is no longer 'social distance' between us and God. God chose to dwell with us in Christ in order that we might be one with one another and one with God. Coming to us as a child, and ascending as an adult, after the resurrection, the unity expressed is that our life is now bound up with God's life.

Bringing about the kingdom of God is therefore what Christian faith is about. It is not supposed to be the Church Preservation Society (good work though such bodies undoubtedly do for our heritage and spirituality). Christianity is a faith of touch, and of bonding. If you don't believe me, just look at the sheer numbers of people Jesus touches in the Gospels. Jesus is the body language of God. He sees the unseen; hears the unheard; speaks for the mute and marginalized; touches the untouchable. The incarnation closes the gap between humanity and divinity. In Christ, there is no more social distance between God and the world.

So, what are we learning about the way forward? I know that in these times, many of us want to do more for others – to make this pandemic more bearable, with its stark economic consequences. Few, if any, will be able to escape some impact. There are health concerns – for ourselves and those we care for and love. Jobs are at risk, as are savings and pensions. Social and physical distancing is testing.

In a few months, this pandemic dramatically altered societies. Covid-19 penetrated every culture, class, region and race; and regardless of religious affiliation, sexuality or gender. It devastated social relations, dismantling ways of expressing warmth and welcome, cruelly robbing mourners of rituals of bereavement and the ability to seek comfort among friends and family – all in our efforts to stem the spread of the virus.

This unthinkable scale of loss, the dramatic measures implemented to prevent further losses, and the vacuum this has left in most of our 'social lives', in their broadest and most vital sense, has resulted in a collective experience of trauma and grief. There is much private suffering. There is and shall be enormous structural suffering.

In the midst of this, I expect that you, like me, will have been inspired by stories of medical and care staff bravely and selflessly protecting the public and paying with their lives. And of neighbourhood and community schemes working overtime to care for the isolated and our most vulnerable. Of charities that have stepped in to unforeseen gaps of provision and care. Those at the forefront of care and charity will continue to need our support long after the immediate repercussions of this pandemic are past.

The pandemic demanded strength, courage and imagination. Our best resources always lie within us, and are among those closest to us, our communities and colleagues. We as a nation began to learn valuable lessons. That the primary purpose of government and leadership is to protect lives, not the economy. Care comes before cash; lives before livelihoods. We would only get ahead of the virus if we put people first. We would have to live differently if we were to beat the virus rather than follow in its wake.

In the meantime, we are on our own road to Emmaus. Just

as two unnamed disciples found (Luke 24.13–35), Jesus' resurrection *re-minds* us – it changes the way we think and act. As we witness him who was dead, breaking bread before us, we must look forward, not merely backwards.

Now, all over the world, we are being *re-minded* and, in the recovery of memory, *re-membering*. But this is no longer just an act of recollection. Rather, *re-membering* is putting things back together that should not have been taken apart; and putting things together anew – to make a better world.

So, communities mobilized and acted where the state cannot function well, if at all. Aid packages, food parcels, spare and vacant flats for healthcare workers were part of this. People rediscovered service to their neighbours, communities and those who cannot care for themselves. Community drivers, babysitting networks for children of key workers, new ways of teaching, playing and relaxing were all being born. In one city, a 'Mums on the Run' group jogged to fetch medicines for those isolated at home. Without a hint of irony, they re-christened themselves as the 'Drug Runners'.

We began to learn some new ways of living as a result of these challenges. A truly charitable heart and a giving attitude is powerful and unstoppable when it is wedded to serious spiritual and social intelligence. We might have been socially distant from one another at the time, but we were not apart.

Easter calls us to the core of our commitment. We are *bonded* together in faith, hope and love. We are bonded together to *re-member* this world of Christ's, as God would piece it back together. To *re-mind* the world that resurrection changes our moral and social order. Knitted together in acts of charity, love, service and sacrifice, we discover touching places between our humanity and God's divinity; between solitude and society. Standing in the midst of this is the resurrected Christ – the sign of God's overwhelming abundant love and grace that we are bidden to accept and then offer to all. As Archbishop Justin has said:

Once this epidemic is conquered, we cannot be content to go back to what was before as if all was normal ... there needs to be a resurrection of our common life, a new normal, something that links to the old but is different and more beautiful.

Indeed. Christ is risen.

Thawing

EMMA PERCY

Narnia, we are told, was a land of snow and ice,
always winter, never Christmas.
Evil was beguiling;
with sweetmeats and vague promises of power.

When the thaw begins
the snow turns to slush,
the paths become muddy,
and potholes are revealed.
The sledges no longer run smoothly.
Journeys need to be rethought
as ice melts and rivers flow.
It is not surprising that there is a hankering for the snow.

Walking through the mud, fording the rivers,
is, at times, heavy going.
Yet, on stumbling, your eye is drawn to fresh shoots
and in the clearing, snowdrops.
There is once again the promise of verdant pastures,
flower-filled meadows, fruitful orchards.
For now, there is mud – but, also snowdrops.

Leaving It to God:
A Sermon for St Matthias

Readings: Psalm 80; 1 Samuel 16.1–13;
Matthew 7.19–27

MARTYN PERCY

Sometimes we choose the readings for a sermon and sometimes they choose us. St Matthias is the apostle who replaced Judas and was chosen by means of lottery to take the number of disciples back up to 12. But before we talk about Matthias, we need a word about the two deaths we remember from Holy Week. Noting that on Good Friday and after the death of Jesus, all the disciples dispersed and ran away, one modern poet, Norma Farber ('Compassion'), asks where we might find Mary, the mother of Jesus on that day:

> In Mary's house the mourners gather.
> Sorrow pierces them like a nail.
> Where's Mary herself meanwhile?
> Gone to comfort Judas's mother.[1]

As the mystics say, you cannot find Jesus in heaven on Good Friday because he's gone looking for Judas in hell. Jesus won't go home without him. So Judas is the permanent resident elephant in the room for St Matthias' Day. Judas casts a shadow over these readings, and so we cannot ignore him.

Judas is a betrayer. In Dante's *Inferno*, Judas occupies a

podium finish with Brutus and Cassius in the inner, ninth ring of hell. These arch-betrayers of classical antiquity represent treachery. Judas remains a relevant figure today. Everyone will have some taste of treachery; of being the victim of others bearing false witness; of being snared; of being badly let down by someone you had trusted. I have that experience. So do many of you. We have known the false kiss; the deceiving smile-charm grin to your face, yet the knife in the back.

Consider Gethsemane. Judas was concealing the financial accounts from the other disciples and stealing too. But don't worry, in our modern rendering of this parable, the Church of England convened a Safeguarding Core Group. It has concluded that Judas meant no harm by his actions. Judas didn't actually take any money from Jesus. There will be a 'lessons learned' review. Judas' ministry can therefore continue.

When you think about it, there is quite a bit of gambling going on in the Bible. Pilate offers the crowd baying for blood a 50–50 choice – do you want Jesus or Barabbas? Even though it is a 50–50 'ask the audience' eliminator, the odds, we sense, are already firmly stacked against Jesus. Before he is crucified, Jesus is blindfolded and invited to guess who struck him. It is a kind of cruel wager, in which all odds are stacked against the victim. We all know what it is like to see the person who might strike you, but we are left befuddled when it is a shadowy group, committee or process. At the end of the Gospels, the soldiers draw lots for Jesus' clothes. So at the foot of the cross, the executioners and guards play dice before God.

But there are other odds too. What are the odds of a small Jewish sect becoming the world's largest faith? No one took a punt at Ladbrokes on that one in AD 33. What were the odds that a key member of the disciples' team, and the treasurer no less, would lose his place to an unknown man named Matthias – the disciple chosen to replace Judas, and chosen by lottery? Two names put before the panel to consider, but only one is chosen, the preferred candidate ...

Let's talk about Matthias. I like the story of Matthias, because it shows, for starters, that the first Christians were actually quite Anglican. That is to say, they knew the value of being pragmatic and could put it before principle when needed. I suppose the better thing to do with Judas' successor was to go into a lockdown conclave and emerge only when ready. But time is short; there is a mission to get on with. They need a twelfth apostle – preferably before supper and sunset – and so they draw lots. It's a gamble. Yet it seems to pay off.

But there is a deeper theme at work in the manner of Matthias' selection that is reflected in both the Old and the New Testament readings, and it is this: we are all dispensable. As Karl Barth noted, the history within the Scriptures also conceals God's parable. In *The Humanity of God*, Barth writes:

> It remains true that God, as creator and Lord of [us], is always free to produce even in human activity and its results, in spite of the problems involved, *parables* of his eternal good will and actions. It is more than ever true, then, that with regard to these no proud abstention but only reverence, joy and gratitude are appropriate.[2]

So, reverence, joy and gratitude are what we strive for, even in the midst of pain, darkness, suffering and injustice. God's work is not *only* accomplished through us. It was done through your predecessors, and will be continued through your successors. Matthias is patron saint of 'It Doesn't All Depend on You'. Judas is airbrushed out of history, and now an unknown runner called Matthias reminds us that God is not lacking on the supply side for people to work with, provided they are committed to joy, gratitude and true service. Be that person.

Because God does know a thing or two about the odds of his purpose being worked out. And I would not bet against the outcome. God does not ask us to gamble. Merely to remember that there are no reliable odds on how your future will turn out. But the God of the present – and of the future – will not let you down. So we do not need to live as others might, because the 'citizenship of heaven', as Paul calls it, will see that we are in the end held and cherished by a God who will not let us fall.

I think Matthias might have agreed with Woody Allen: 'If you want to make God laugh, tell him your future plans.' Most people know the so-called 'Serenity Prayer' – or at least the first part of it. Very few, however, know that the original was written by Reinhold Niebuhr in the darkest days of World War Two. The prayer goes like this: 'God, grant me grace to accept with serenity the things that cannot be changed; courage to change the things which should be changed; and the wisdom to know the difference ...'

But the prayer then continues:

... living one day at a time, enjoying one moment at a time, accepting hardship as a pathway to peace; and taking, as Jesus did, this sinful world as it is. Not as I would have it, but trusting that you will make all things right, if I but surrender to your will. So that I may be reasonably happy in this life; and supremely happy with you forever, in the next ...

Many soldiers were given this prayer as they left America for Europe; or England for Normandy on D-Day.

That's the point, surely. God hears the prayer from the trenches; he hears the prayer of the ones rooting for a successor to Judas. But God knows life can be fickle and ever-changing. Because God has already become one of us. He has loved us enough to live for us, as one of us, and among us. He has known what it is to have the odds stacked against him. He has risked that enough to die as one of us – and yet be raised up.

Anyway, perhaps I should say something about our readings by way of closing. Our psalm is unequivocal: God will save and restore, and even though our detractors may scorn us and laugh at us, God will never turn away from you. Never. The anointing of David from 1 Samuel 16 reminds us that God often chooses the runt of the litter – the littlest and the lesser is where God begins. It is what Jesus starts his ministry with, time and time again. God is always looking for the outsider to confound the insider; the least to be the greatest; the gentle to show the strong how to be; the foolish to convert the wise.

David is picked because he's no Goliath. He is a minor character put out to tend flocks and amuses himself by making up the songs and tunes we know as psalms. God likes to do extraordinary things with the neglected and the rejected. God chooses the weak and the foolish things of the world to confound the wise and strong. God grows the fruit of his Spirit within our yielding flesh, hearts and minds. Growing fruit is slow work. Cheap, false piety that mimics authentic growth will always be available in plentiful quantities. But discerning disciples are seldom fooled by such offerings. Quality takes time to bud and flower.

Likewise, you can build almost anything, instantly, on sand. But without deep, solid foundations, what is knocked up in the morning is swept away by the evening. Building a solid structure on unforgiving rock, with all the boring into the ground required to establish the foundations, is hard and laborious. But persevere. Slow church is where we find God slogging away, working with grace, love, goodness, charity, kindness, mercy and endless patience over the decades and centuries. It takes a long, long time to bring the gospel to any community; or to a country. Only fools think this can be fast.

My vocation to serve Christ and the world as priest, pastor and professor will continue. But my season for doing so within the Church of England must now end, so that truth can be spoken to power, and prophetic insight not be diminished by the gravitational pressure of institutional loyalty.

In this, I take my cue from Jonah. Do not look back in anger. Look forward only in love, and by education and example, live for others as Christ does, whether you are an insider or an outsider. As that other famous Dean – James Dean – once said, 'Only the gentle are truly strong.'

We face many challenges in our world today: wars, famine, disease and injustice. Hold fast to God and to one another. Be good. Be humble. God, who is faithful, will not let you fall. 'Do not be afraid' and 'Do not fear' are phrases most often repeated by Jesus in the Gospels – more than 70 times. Our calling does not seek safety, security or any other benefits. Our vocation is not to cling to church, but rather to step out in the love revealed in the person of Jesus.

For me, and you, that is the path that now lies ahead. May God grant us all grace and peace, as we walk with him who is ever beside and before us. Amen.

Notes

1 Norma Farber, 'Compassion', in *Something Further: Poems*, New York: Kylix Press, 1979, p. 27. Norma Farber was born in 1909 and died in 1984.

2 Karl Barth, *The Humanity of God*, Louisville, KY: Westminster John Knox Press, 1956, p. 84.

Closing Prayers

Resurrection life

Some say I'm brave, God. Others say I'm strong.
Really, I just have no choice.
I have to keep moving forward, otherwise what is left?
I have to turn this pain into something powerful, otherwise
what is it for?
I have to make something positive out of this mess, otherwise
why survive it?

Father, Mother, Jesus, Spirit, Wisdom, Prophet, Yeshua.
Come to me today as I need you to be.
Let us co-create the next step in our journey of life.
Give me what I need to be your hands today. Your voice,
your words on a screen, your persistent presence in the park,
the corner shop, the twittersphere.
Thank you for the free will you give me so I may joyfully give
my life back to you.
Thank you for the opportunities you present me with so I can
turn my suffering into singing.

Thank you for being here with me on the days when my
sadness is too overwhelming. I know you understand.
As close to me as the breath which enters my lungs and leaves
them purified.
Thank you for the bravery you give me, the strength you
empower me with, the choice that you present me with, so
I can move forward, transform my pain and enter into the
resurrection life with you.
Amen.

We will not stop

We will not stop, nor should we.
Until heaven is here on earth and we live in the kin-dom
of God.
Until radical inclusivity is no longer radical, and the diversity
of God's design is celebrated.
Until lives are no longer sacrificed at the altar of toxic
theology and tradition over love.
Until we learn to see each other as God sees us; beloved,
cherished, each and every single one.

A prayer of thanksgiving

Thank you for the Jarrow Marchers, who would not let
poverty stand and did something about it.

Thank you for visionary figures such as William Booth
and Shirley Chisholm, who actively challenged the status
quo and worked to make life better for those in poverty in
their lifetimes.

Thank you for the multitude of charitable organizations
providing relief in the space beyond where the government's
provision ends.

Thank you for poverty activists such as Jack Monroe, Martin
Lewis, Marcus Rashford and others who protest at great
personal cost, yet keep on doing so for the sake of the poorest
among us.

Thank you for those unnamed individuals who give of their
personal time each and every day, to care and contribute in
their local communities.

Thank you for stirring our hearts in the name of social justice.
In the name of loving our neighbours.

As we look to the examples of those who have gone before, those who work today, those who need our help. We say. 'Here I am. Take me.'

For as long as I am needed

For as long as I am needed I will serve you, O my God.
For as long as there is injustice I will not be still.
For as long as there is pain I will share your love.
For as long as there is need I will seek to meet it.
For as long as there is despair I will be a beacon of your hope.
For as long as I am needed, God, until your kin-dom comes.
Amen.

A daily prayer

Give me a hunger for justice, Jesus
A hunger which matches your own.
Give me a relentless spirit which searches for truth.

Give me a thirst for love, Jesus
A thirst which can never be quenched.
Give me a generosity to share it far and wide.

Give me a gift of connection, Jesus
A gift which can only grow.
Give me the means to use it wherever I go.

Give me the peace of your Spirit, Jesus
The peace which allows me to rest.
Long may I rest in your presence when each day is done.

Amen.